The Pope Francis Agenda:
His Teaching on Family, Protection of Life,
Justice, Ecology, Women & the Church

THE
POPE FRANCIS
AGENDA

His Teaching on Family,
Protection of Life, Justice, Ecology,
Women & the Church

DONAL DORR

VERITAS

Published 2018 by Veritas Publications
7–8 Lower Abbey Street
Dublin 1, Ireland
publications@veritas.ie
www.veritas.ie

ISBN 978 1 84730 839 9

10 9 8 7 6 5 4 3 2 1

A catalogue record for this book is available from the British Library.

Cover designed by Heather Costello, Veritas Publications
Author photograph by Zoe Ardiff
Printed in the Republic of Ireland by Walsh Colour Print, Co. Kerry

*Veritas books are printed on paper made from the wood pulp of managed
forests. For every tree felled, at least one tree is planted, thereby renewing
natural resources.*

With deep gratitude, and just a little trepidation, I dedicate this book to some of the many women who have inspired, empowered, supported and challenged me over many years:

My sister Ben Kimmerling and my sisters-in-law Eileen Lynch and Caitriona Doran; several friends – Berne Okure, Barbara Linen, Marian Lohman, Ellen Alma, Ntombi Nyathi, Mary O'Callaghan, Imelda Smyth, Kathy Tyler, and Julie Brennan, as well as the members of the APT (Act to Prevent Trafficking) group; and some friends who have already completed this stage of our earthly journey – Anne Hope, Helena Brennan, Jean Eason, Maura O'Donohue, Miriam O'Brian, Maura Ramsbottom and Mary Guy.

I hope I've heard your voices.

Contents

SECTION THREE
INTEGRAL SOCIAL TEACHING

BIBLIOGRAPHY

Introduction

One of the more striking and plaintive statements of Jesus in the Gospels is: 'Can you not discern the signs of the times?' (Mt 16:3). That question comes as a *warning* to all of us today, living as we do in a world marked by very high levels of injustice and exploitation – one in which scientists suggest that our present lifestyle is quite unsustainable. But for Christians, the plea also comes as an exciting *invitation* to recognise that, right before our eyes, something radically new is taking place in our Church. We Christians are living now in a *kairos* time, a key moment of history, one offering a creative opportunity for something quite new and fresh to emerge in the way we experience, and understand, and live out our Christian faith in the Catholic Church. And Jesus is asking us plaintively to recognise the need for such a radical and exciting change – and to embrace it and to play our part in bringing it about.

The Church is, of course, a community of committed believers. But it is also a very large institution in which it is by no means easy to bring about change. When change does come it usually begins at the margins and only gradually seeps inwards and upwards to affect the senior authorities. One thinks, for instance, of the quite radical new spirituality brought into the Church by St Francis of Assisi, St Clare, and their companions. But it would seem that, at two key moments in the recent life of our Church, God saw that the problems were so urgent and intractable that the usual process of percolation from the margins was not sufficient. So, at each of these two *kairos* moments God chose to bring about change 'from the top down', choosing a pope as a key instrument of radical change.

The first of these *kairos* moments came in the early weeks of the Second Vatican Council when Pope John XXIII chose to stand firmly on the side of those bishops who challenged the attempt of the Vatican insiders to control the process of the council and its outcome. The result of Pope John's radical stance unfolded over the following years when we Catholics, along with many other Christians, woke up to a fresh and liberating experience of what it means to be a Christian believer. We found that a burden had been lifted from our shoulders, a yoke from our necks (cf. Is 10:27) – one that most of us had so taken for granted that we only became aware of it as we were being led into the freedom of the children of God.

Unfortunately, there were still quite a lot of Church leaders who, from the beginning, resisted this change. And over the following fifty years they were succeeded by others who were fearful of change and who wished to retain their power. They succeeded to a very considerable extent in playing down the more radical implications of the Vatican Council.

This second *kairos* began with the radically courageous decision of Pope Benedict XVI to resign. It came into bloom with the election of Pope Francis. The new pope immediately signalled a break with the past by taking the name Francis. He came on to the balcony of St Peter's describing himself as the Bishop of Rome, rather than as pope, and asking the people to bless him and pray for him. In this way he indicated that he was adopting a different style and a different agenda from

Pope John Paul II and Pope Benedict XVI. From the beginning this different style was quite evident; and in the years since his election his particular agenda has been revealed incrementally.

Ironically, this 'different' agenda is in fact very much a return to all that Vatican II represented. However, it is much more than a literal application of the words of the key documents of the council. Francis has fully embraced what has been called 'the spirit of Vatican II'. This involves being open to the spirit and to the emergence of new insights not only in the Church but in the wider world, insights which give us a fresh understanding of what it means to live as Christians *today*, fifty years after the council. Francis spelled this out very clearly in his address to the members of the Italian Theological Association on 29 December 2017. There he said that the Church has the responsibility 'to proclaim the Gospel in a new way, one that is more appropriate to a world and a culture that has radically changed'; and he spoke of the need for theologians especially to have 'a creative faithfulness'.

In this book I have set out to document the unfolding of the many dimensions of the agenda of Pope Francis up to April 2018. Some outstanding elements in this agenda are his new teaching on ecology, his unabashed embrace of key elements of liberation theology, his sharp critique of clericalism, and his sustained efforts to move towards a more decentralised and synodal model of Church governance. While spelling out these significant changes in his *teaching*, I have also tried to communicate some sense of his radically new *style* which must be seen as just as important.

In the subtitle of the book I have used the phrase 'teaching' for a reason. My understanding of 'teaching' in this context extends further than the formal teaching found in his official documents. It also includes the somewhat less formal teaching in his many speeches and his official messages and letters to various agencies and individuals. I have also included much of his informal teaching in the dialogues and planned conversations in which he engaged with journalists and others, as well as in his Sunday morning talks from the balcony of St Peter's. I have even referred at times to things he has said in more informal conversations and in his homilies at morning Masses. In the case of Pope Francis, it is quite clear that all of these form a coherent unity.

This book is not just about the official *teaching* of Pope Francis. My hope is that I shall also succeed in conveying a flavour of the *spirituality* which he lives and preaches. I would have wanted to insert the word 'spirituality' alongside the word 'teaching' in the subtitle of the book; but this would have made the subtitle unduly long.

The sheer volume of the writings and speeches of Pope Francis make it obvious that much of this material has been drafted for him by friends and colleagues who work very closely with him. However, the frequency with which he speaks in an ad-lib manner makes it equally obvious that he never 'parrots' material that has been prepared for him by others. It is evident that his speech-writers and those who draft his written material have succeeded in articulating what he himself wants to say or to write. So he fully 'owns' all of this material. For this reason I find it unnecessary to attempt the almost impossible task of discovering who drafted any of his material. I assume that all of it represents 'the real Pope Francis'.

Introduction

On numerous occasions Francis has made it clear that he is in favour of having open and respectful dialogue in the Church. He believes it is important that different viewpoints on important Church issues should be aired. He has also said that he himself welcomes being challenged. For instance, in his dialogue with the leaders of congregations of religious women in May 2016, he thanked them for their courage in questioning a practice in the Church which they considered to be unjust, and said that he likes being questioned.

In this book I have taken Francis at his word on this issue of questioning and challenging. So I have not hesitated to point out some areas where responsible commentators feel it is important to question his views or his actions. This applies in regard to the issue of clerical sex abuse, to the issue of his views on the role of women in the Church, and even in regard to some relatively minor details of his extraordinarily important ecological encyclical. In pointing out areas where I think there is need for change I have tried to be respectful and to ensure that any criticism I make does not detract from my enthusiastic approval of his achievements and his overall agenda.

Some of the chapters – particularly those that deal with the teaching of Pope Francis on ecology and justice – draw on material I wrote two years ago as one small part of my major study of Catholic social teaching over the past one hundred and twenty-five years. This larger book, *Option for the Poor and for the Earth: From Leo XIII to Pope Francis*, was published by Orbis Books, Maryknoll, USA in 2016. It was written and laid out as a textbook, mainly for university students in American Catholic universities. The sheer size of that book (over five hundred pages) and its relatively high cost means that only a small number of copies have been sold on this side of the Atlantic. So I decided, with the agreement of Orbis, to use an adapted and updated version of that material here in order to make it available to readers on this side of the pond.

The present book has a large amount of new material, including a treatment of the important teaching of Pope Francis on marriage, abortion, homosexuality, the role of discernment and conscience, liturgy, women in the Church, and on the issues of peace-making, non-violence, and the unacceptability of capital punishment. Because what Pope Francis has to say about ecological issues is perhaps the most original and significant aspect of his teaching, I have decided to locate my treatment of this topic in a separate series of chapters – chapters twelve to twenty-two.

I have no hesitation in claiming that Pope Francis has made a major contribution to Catholic social teaching. So, towards the end of this book I have included two chapters about Catholic social teaching, as it stands now, in the light of the new directions and emphasis which he has given to that teaching. Equally important, I believe that Francis has greatly enriched the faith experience and spirituality of enormous numbers of Christians. Furthermore, his actions, his words, and his style have led many governments and very many non-Christians to see the Church in a far more favourable light than they had in the past.

I am delighted that Veritas has undertaken to publish this book, because I have a sense that, even though most people in this country respond positively to him, there are many, even among committed Catholics, who do not have a good understanding of the radical new model of Christianity for which Pope Francis stands. My hope is that the book will help a wide readership to appreciate the remarkable contribution he is making to the Catholic Church and to the wider world.

Donal Dorr
11 April 2018

Section One

RENEWAL AND CHALLENGE FROM
THE TOP DOWN

Chapter One

A New Approach: Joy and Mercy

Although there has been considerable continuity in Catholic social teaching over the years since Leo XIII's great encyclical *Rerum Novarum* of 1891, different popes have at times shifted the emphasis in significant ways. Perhaps the most dramatic of these changes came in 1961, when John XXIII effectively proposed the kind of welfare state which his predecessors had considered quite unacceptable. The Vatican Council (1962–5) went on to abandon the idea that 'error has no rights' and made major developments in Church teaching about respect for conscience and for other Christians and other religions. It made a radical change in the Church's approach to the relationship between the Church and the state. In doing so it opened a space for the emergence, a few years later, of liberation theology and spirituality, as well as feminist theology, and an integration of the insights of modern humanistic psychology into Catholic spirituality.

Much more recently Pope Benedict XVI sought to make another shift of emphasis in Catholic social teaching by playing down the theology of liberation which had posed a very radical challenge to the capitalist system of economy. Instead, he highlighted the importance of an 'economy of communion' through which the capitalist system could be gradually transformed and humanised.

With Pope Francis has come yet another shift of emphasis. Indeed, there is a strong case for saying that his approach involves perhaps even more than a shift of emphasis. As Leonardo Boff says: 'There are no better words to describe this than the terms *break and beginning anew*' (Boff 2014, 7). In this book I am offering a quite detailed account of the many different elements in this break with the past, while also recognising the extent to which Francis remains true to past teaching – above all to the teaching and spirit of the Second Vatican Council. In doing so, I draw on a great variety of papal and Vatican documents. But I rely especially on the four major documents issued by Pope Francis. The first of these is his apostolic exhortation, *Evangelii Gaudium* ('The Joy of the Gospel'), issued on 24 November 2013. The second is his major encyclical, *Laudato Si': On Care for Our Common Home,* dated 24 May 2015, in which he urges us to hear 'the cry of the earth and the cry of the poor'. The third is his apostolic exhortation on marriage and the family, *Amoris Laetitia* ('The Joy of Love'), dated 19 March 2016. I have also referred quite a lot to two very significant and radical speeches he made to activists in what are called 'popular movements'. He gave the first of these in Rome on 28 October 2014 and the second in Bolivia on 9 July 2015. On 10 November 2017 Francis gave an important speech about nuclear weapons.

Each of these documents and speeches spells out in some detail one or more of the major issues which together constitute what I am calling 'the Pope Francis Agenda'. These issues include the encouragement of active resistance to the present model of so-called development, the urgent need for care of the earth, the protection of human life at every stage from conception to death, peace-making, and the need for reform in the institutional Church.

In *Evangelii Gaudium*, hereafter referred to as *EG*, Francis presents Christians with what he calls his 'dream' (*EG,* 27). In fact this document can be seen as a kind of manifesto – the vision that he aims to see lived out in the Church and in the lives of Christians. The Pope's address of 28 October 2014 is a cry of outrage about the present unjust situation in our world and offers positive encouragement from Francis to his friends in these movements to continue their crucial work of empowering poor and marginalised people in their struggle to bring about a more just world.

Another apostolic exhortation by Francis, dated 19 March 2018, is called *Gaudete et Exsultate* ('Rejoice and be Glad'). This document differs from the others in not treating in any detail any new item on the action agenda of the Pope. Instead it puts forward a deeply personal and moving account by Francis of the range of attitudes and virtues which should characterise the genuine Christian. The subtitle of the document is 'On the Call to Holiness in Today's World'. This indicates that the agenda of Francis is not just an invitation to us to address such practical issues as care for the earth and the poor, and reform of Church structures and practices. He is equally concerned about the mindset and attitude with which we approach all of these issues; and that is what he is addressing in this exhortation. However, there are elements in this document which can be seen as further elaboration and defence by Francis of the controversial stances he has taken on two contentious issues; the first of these is whether the Church's opposition to abortion should take absolute priority over every other situation where human life is threatened (see chapter three); the second is how best pastors should respond in a truly merciful way to people who are divorced and remarried (see chapter two).

JOY

For previous popes the key word in Catholic social teaching was 'solidarity'. Francis, too, sees this concept as crucial. But for him, in everything he says and writes, the words which take pride of place are 'joy' and 'mercy'. It is significant that in the titles of his major documents there are three different versions of the word 'joy'. 'Joy' is not merely in the title of *Evangelii Gaudium* but is also a fundamental theme of the document (cf. *EG*, 2–8). Joy is present in the title of his ecology encyclical, *Laudato Si'* (24 May 2015), since the word 'laudato' denotes a surge of joyful praise rather than a more sober compliment or tribute. Francis chose to put another Latin word for joy into the title of his major document about marriage and family, *Amoris Laetitia*, issued on 19 March 2016. And, as if to put even more emphasis on joy, Francis chose two words signifying joy as the title for his March 2018 apostolic exhortation, *Gaudete et Exsultate*. He also put the emphasis on joy in his Message for Mission Sunday 2014 (2–3), and in very many of his addresses and homilies.

In a moving passage towards the end of *Evangelii Gaudium* Francis invites his readers to follow Jesus by entering 'fully into the fabric of society, sharing the lives of all, listening to their concerns, helping them materially and spiritually in their needs, rejoicing with those who rejoice, weeping with those who weep'. He adds that as we go 'arm in arm with others, we are committed to building a new world', and 'we do so not from a sense of obligation, not as a burdensome duty, but as the result of a personal decision which brings us joy and gives meaning to our lives' (*EG*, 269).

In *Gaudete et Exsultate* there are forty-six locations where he uses the word 'joy' or words such as 'joyful' or 'enjoy'. He says: 'Far from being timid, morose, acerbic or melancholy, or putting on a dreary face, the saints are joyful and full of good humour. Though completely realistic, they radiate a positive and hopeful spirit' (*GE*, 122). Francis then goes on to offer a comprehensive scriptural and theological account of joy (*GE*, 122–8). These are paragraphs which deserve to be reflected on and prayed over. Francis links humour with joy; and in note 101 he quotes a striking prayer of St Thomas More, of which the key words are: 'Grant me, O Lord, a sense of good humour. Allow me the grace to be able to take a joke and to discover in life a bit of joy, and to be able to share it with others.'

MERCY

It would be no exaggeration to say that *mercy* has been the primary theme of the papacy of Pope Francis. Time after time he has stressed the importance of mercy as a fundamental Christian virtue. The high point was, of course, his jubilee year of mercy. This was announced by him on 13 March 2015, formally proclaimed on 11 April of that year in his document *Misericordiae Vultus*, and ran from 8 December 2015 to 20 November 2016. In that document he said:

> Mercy is the very foundation of the Church's life. All of her
> pastoral activity should be caught up in the tenderness she

makes present to believers; nothing in her preaching and in her witness to the world can be lacking in mercy. The Church's very credibility is seen in how she shows merciful and compassionate love. (*MV*, 10)

As this passage indicates, for Francis the word 'mercy' is primarily a feeling of *tenderness* rather than a more cerebral judgement. In Cuba, during his homily at the shrine of Our Lady of Charity in El Cobre, Santiago, on 22 September 2015, he went so far as to call for his audience to live a 'revolution of tenderness'.

The insistence by Francis on the importance of mercy does not mean that he sees mercy as replacing justice and law. But in his statements, his responses to difficult questions, and above all in his spontaneous actions, he has made it clear that it is not enough for Church leaders or for any Christian to insist on laying down laws or principles. For him there is a delicate balance to be preserved: on the one hand, Christians are called to hold onto, and proclaim, the basic principles of Catholic social teaching, but, on the other hand, they must not apply these principles in a rigid take-it-or-leave-it manner. He holds that, in seeking to implement Catholic social teaching as well as all other aspects of Church teaching, it is essential that Christian leaders do so with sensitivity and respect, taking account of the real-life situations of those with whom they are dealing and always keeping in mind the fundamental Christian belief in the compassion and mercy of God.

A striking instance of the belief and teaching of Pope Francis on this issue of compassion and flexibility comes in the address he gave at the conclusion of the Synod on the Family. While acknowledging that dogmatic questions are clearly defined by the magisterium, he pointed out that cultures are quite diverse and that 'every general principle needs to be inculturated, if it is to be respected and applied'. He said that the experience of the Synod of Bishops 'made us better realise that the true defenders of doctrine are not those who uphold its letter, but its spirit'. In a quite sharp rebuke to those who are unduly rigid upholders of the law, he said that the synod 'was about bearing witness to everyone that, for the Church, the Gospel continues to be a vital source of eternal newness, against all those who would "indoctrinate" it in dead stones to be hurled at others'. Speaking about the Synod, he insisted:

> It was also about laying bare closed hearts which frequently hide even behind the Church's teachings or good intentions, in order to sit in the chair of Moses and judge, sometimes with superiority and superficiality, difficult cases and wounded families ... It was about trying to open up broader horizons, rising above conspiracy theories and blinkered viewpoints, so as to defend and spread the freedom of the children of God, and to transmit the beauty of Christian Newness, at times encrusted in a language which is archaic or simply incomprehensible. (24 October 2015)

Pope Francis himself is a good model of how to combine strong condemnation of social evils with a non-judgemental attitude in relation to the individual person. In his interview for the Jesuit magazines he said: 'During the return flight from Rio de Janeiro I said that if a homosexual person is of good will and is in

25

search of God, I am no one to judge.' He then went on to say: 'A person once asked me, in a provocative manner, if I approved of homosexuality. I replied with another question: "Tell me: when God looks at a gay person, does he endorse the existence of this person with love, or reject and condemn this person?" We must always consider the person' (interview with Spadaro, 2013).

The priority which Francis gives to mercy is the most distinctive feature of his document, *Amoris Laetitia*, on marriage and the family, issued on 19 March 2016. The word 'mercy' occurs thirty-seven times in this document. Indeed the whole document might well be described as 'an invitation to mercy and pastoral discernment' (*AL*, 6). He wants all Christians 'to experience being touched by an "unmerited, unconditional and gratuitous mercy"' (*AL*, 297). He tartly insists that he does not want pastors 'to apply moral laws to those living in "irregular" situations, as if they were stones to throw at people's lives' (*AL*, 305). He goes on to say that he wants 'the balm of mercy to reach everyone, believers and those far away' (*AL*, 309). He protests against those who, he says, water down the Gospel by putting so many conditions on mercy that it is 'emptied of its concrete meaning and real significance' (*AL*, 311). And in the same paragraph he even goes so far as to maintain that 'mercy is the fullness of justice and the most radiant manifestation of God's truth'. This statement of Francis represents a sharp corrective to some of those who, in prioritising the 'Divine Mercy' devotion, perhaps take too literally the statement of St Faustina that the present time of mercy will be followed by a time of justice. It is clear that, for Pope Francis, mercy rather than justice has, so to speak, 'the last word'.

The insistence of Francis on the priority of mercy led him to suggest in *Amoris Laetitia* that divorced people who have married again could in certain circumstances by allowed to receive Holy Communion (cf. *AL,* footnote 351). His stance on this issue has aroused resistance and rejection by a relatively small but articulate group, including even some cardinals and bishops. But it has not led him to change his position. This is an issue which I shall treat more fully in the next chapter.

In his 2018 apostolic exhortation *Gaudete et Exsultate* Francis spells out what it means for a Christian to practise mercy in everyday life. He says it means seeing Christ in people who are poor or suffering, following the instruction of Jesus himself in the Gospel of Matthew (*GS,* 95–9).

Earlier in the same exhortation he has an extended treatment of the theology and spirituality of grace (*GE,* 52–62). In this section of the document he is in fact providing the basis for his strong emphasis throughout his teaching on the centrality of mercy. He says: 'The Church has repeatedly taught that we are justified not by our own works or efforts, but by the grace of the Lord, who always takes the initiative' (*GE,* 52). So we are invited 'to live in joyful gratitude for this completely unmerited gift'. Francis then quotes a statement of St Thérèse of the Child Jesus in which she says to God: 'All our justices have stains in your sight' (*GE,* 54). So we must rely on the mercy of God rather than on our own achievements. Francis goes on to say:

> We do well to keep reminding ourselves that there is a hierarchy of virtues that bids us seek what is essential. The primacy belongs to the theological virtues, which have

God as their object and motive. At the centre is charity ...
Jesus ... gives us two faces, or better yet, one alone: the face
of God reflected in so many other faces. For in every one
of our brothers and sisters, especially the least, the most
vulnerable, the defenceless and those in need, God's very
image is found. (*GE*, 61–2)

Chapter Two

Care for the Family: *Amoris Laetitia*

Pope Francis is deeply concerned about what is happening at the present time to the most fundamental structure of society, namely, the family. That is why he chose to convene a two-phase Synod of Bishops on this topic in the years 2014 and 2015. In sharp contrast to what had taken place during synods over the previous twenty years, he encouraged the participants to engage in uninhibited dialogue and debate, even when this led to very sharp disagreement.

On 19 March 2016, the document *Amoris Laetitia* ('The Joy of Love'), on marriage and the family, was issued by Francis as his response to the Synod. It is remarkably practical and pastoral in tone. Although it is in fundamental doctrinal continuity with previous Church teaching, there is a quite distinct shift of emphasis. While taking account of the *objective* rightness or wrongness of specific activities, Francis focuses attention more particularly on the *subjective* aspect of morality where the role of discernment and personal conscience are of crucial importance.

The first chapter of this key document gives us a short reflection by Francis on what happened during the two sessions of the Synod on marriage and family. Perhaps his most important comment here is his criticism of the debate which took place in some publications and the media. He says that some commentators had 'an attitude that would solve everything by applying general rules or deriving undue conclusions from particular theological considerations'. This remark alerts us to the fact that one of the main aims of Francis in this document; he is inviting us to move beyond such an attitude and take account of the individual circumstances of each person and the personal discernment which has to take place in the light of each particular situation.

In the second chapter of the document, Francis confronts the specific problems faced by married couples and families at the present time. The third chapter explores the light which Jesus throws on marriage and the family. It then goes on to reflect rather briefly on the teaching of Scripture and tradition on marriage. Francis then refers to 'imperfect situations' where a couple are living in 'an irregular union'. He speaks of 'the Church's pastoral care for the faithful who are living together, or are only married civilly, or are divorced and remarried'.

The fourth chapter is significant because it is a particularly striking example of the fact that Pope Francis bases his moral teaching more on *virtue* than on *law* (cf. Lawler and Todd 2017, 586). In pre-Vatican times, the treatment of Catholic moral theology manuals was generally based on the commandments and on Church law. Even after the council this law-based approach continued in a less rigid way in much of official Vatican teaching on moral issues. But over the past fifty years many moral theologians had moved to what came to be called 'a virtue ethics'. Francis adopts this approach in a particularly inspiring way in chapter four of *Amoris Laetitia*. What he offers us is a deeply moving reflection on the nature of genuine love, in which he meditates on the words of St Paul in 1 Corinthians 13:1–13. So he spells out the ways in which love unfolds in the virtues of patience, generosity, forgiveness, endurance, faith, and hope – as well as in a loving service of others which is not jealous, rude, irritable, or resentful. He then goes on to write honestly and movingly about the erotic dimension of love.

In *Gaudete et Exsultate* Francis offers another meditation on Christian virtues, explaining in some detail how we can live the Gospel Beatitudes in everyday life (*GE*, 63–94). He follows this with a moving account of how a Christian should live out the virtue of mercy in practice by recognising and responding to Christ in those who are poor or suffering, as spelled out by Jesus himself in the Gospel of Matthew (*GE*, 95–9).

In chapter five of *Amoris Laetitia* Francis deals with issues relating to the generation of new life and parental love. Then there is a section on love and care for those who are elderly. The sixth chapter addresses practical issues related to preparation for marriage, the ongoing accompaniment of married couples, crisis situations, breakdowns of marriage, and responding to death in the family. The seventh chapter focuses on the education of children, including sex education. In the ninth and final chapter Francis outlines a spirituality of marriage and the family.

CONTROVERSY

The most controversial part of the document is the eighth chapter which is entitled 'Accompanying, Discerning and Integrating Weakness'. In this chapter Francis addresses the crucial issue of pastoral care for people living in various kinds of 'irregular situations'. It is in this section that he inserted a controversial endnote (cf. *AL*, footnote 351) where he suggested, in a rather oblique manner, that it may be acceptable in some circumstances for people who had divorced and remarried to receive Holy Communion.

The position of Francis on this issue seems to conflict with the clear teaching of Pope John Paul II in his 1981 apostolic exhortation *Familiaris Consortio*, where he said that those who are divorced cannot be allowed to receive Holy Communion. This, he said, is because 'their state and condition of life objectively contradict that union of love between Christ and the Church which is signified and effected by the Eucharist' (*FC*, 84).

In the final chapter of *Gaudete et Exsultate* Francis includes an extended treatment of the process of discernment (*GE*, 166–75). He insists that it is 'more than intelligence or common sense'. It is in fact a gift of the Holy Spirit (*GE*, 166). It enables us to read 'the signs of the times' (*GE*, 168). Without it we may fail to heed the promptings of God's grace and disregard God's invitation to grow (*GS*, 169). It is the way in which we seek 'a glimpse of that unique and mysterious plan that God has for each of us' (*GE*, 170).

Francis goes on to say that God speaks to us in a variety of ways; for instance, in our work or though interaction with other people. Nevertheless, 'we simply cannot do without the silence of prolonged prayer, which enables us better to perceive God's language, to interpret the real meaning of the inspirations we believe we have received, to calm our anxieties and to see the whole of our existence afresh in his own light' (*GE*, 171). He adds that we must allow ourselves to 'become truly open to accepting a call that can shatter our security' (*GE*, 172).

It is quite likely that, in writing these paragraphs about discernment, Francis was responding to those who are unwilling to accept the possibility that those who are divorced and remarried may, after a process of careful discernment, be allowed to receive Holy Communion. Particularly relevant is the following passage: 'It is not a matter of applying rules or repeating what was done in the past, since the same solutions are not valid in all circumstances and what was useful in one context may not prove so in another. The discernment of spirits liberates us from rigidity, which has no place before the perennial "today" of the risen Lord' (*GE*, 173).

How are we to explain this difference between the position of Francis and that of his predecessor? To do so we must see that John Paul II based his decision on the objective state of the divorced person. Francis accepts that the *objective* state of the divorced person is not what it should be. But he focuses more on the personal judgement of *conscience* made by the divorced person following a serious *discernment* made with the help of a pastor. That is why we could say that, while his position is in doctrinal continuity with previous Church teaching, it is new in its emphasis on the role of discernment and personal conscience. However, we must add that in fact traditional moral theology has always recognised the fundamental role of conscience and discernment. So what is really new is the way in which Francis has acknowledged that this ancient teaching is applicable in the situation of some divorced people.

John Paul II had added a second reason why a person who is divorced should not be allowed to receive Communion. He said that if the divorced person were allowed to do so 'the faithful would be led into error and confusion regarding the Church's teaching about the indissolubility of marriage'. No doubt Francis was well aware of this danger. But for him the risk of such scandal must at times take second place in view of the vital importance of ensuring that no conscientious Christian is deprived of the help of the sacraments. So, in *Amoris Laetitia* he quoted what he had already said in *Evangelii Gaudium*, that the Eucharist 'is not a prize for the perfect but a powerful medicine and nourishment for the weak'. And he also said: 'I want to remind priests that the confessional must not be a torture chamber, but rather an encounter with the Lord's mercy' (*AL*, 351).

A month after *Amoris Laetitia* was published Francis visited asylum-seekers on the island of Lesbos in Greece. On the return flight he was asked why his reference to the issue of Communion for remarried people was only put in a footnote of his document. He replied quite sharply:

> When I called the first synod, most of the media were concerned with one question: Will the divorced and remarried be able to receive Communion? Since I am not a saint, this was somewhat annoying to me, and even made me a bit sad. Because I think: those media that say all these things, don't they realise that that is not the important issue? … Don't they realise that the shortage of jobs and employment opportunities is forcing fathers and mothers to take two jobs and children to grow up by themselves and not learn how to talk with their mothers and fathers? These are the big issues!

Some would claim that in these remarks Francis was dodging the issue of the difference between his position and that of John Paul II. But a good case can be made for saying that Francis was well aware of the full significance of all that he had said in *Amoris Laetitia*, including that controversial note. But for him this was just one more element in his overall agenda – an agenda which gives a high priority to the situation of those who have been left on the margins of society. And he was refusing to allow himself to be distracted from his pastoral priorities by allowing himself to get bogged down in a polarised theological controversy.

On 29 January 2018, Francis returned again to the issue of the importance of conscience in regard to issues concerning marriage. Speaking to members of the Roman Rota, which is the Church's highest court, he once again emphasised the point that 'conscience assumes a decisive role in the demanding choices that couples must face'. He maintained that the task of Church leaders is to assist engaged couples in building and preserving 'the intimate sanctuary of their Christian conscience' and he pointed out that this means that bishops and priests must work tirelessly 'to enlighten, defend and support the Christian conscience of our people'.

Not long after the publication of *Amoris Laetitia*, the Argentinian bishops issued guidelines in which they accepted that the Pope's document meant that in certain circumstances a divorced and remarried person could receive Holy Communion. On 5 September 2016, Pope Francis sent a letter to the Argentinian bishops in which he praised their interpretation of *Amoris Laetitia* and said bluntly that there are no other valid interpretations of the document. On 5 December 2017 Francis went further. He maintained that the guidelines of the Argentinian bishops and his letter to them are 'authentic teaching'. So he directed that both should be published on the Vatican website and in the *Acta Apostolicae Sedis*, which is the official record of Vatican documents and acts.

FRANCIS DEFENDS AND JUSTIFIES HIS TEACHING

In his apostolic exhortation *Gaudete et Exsultate*, Pope Francis includes an extended and fascinating treatment of what he describes as two seriously distorted understandings of spirituality (*GE*, 35–62). For him, these 'wrong' spiritualities derive from two wrong theologies (in fact two heretical positions). These are gnosticism and pelagianism or semi-pelagianism. In a footnote (33) Francis says that the doctrinal basis for his position is to be found in the letter '*Placuit Deo*' on Certain Aspects of Christian Salvation' which was issued by the Congregation for the Doctrine of the Faith on 22 February 2018. It seems quite likely that in fact Francis himself had asked the members of this Vatican department to write the *Placuit Deo* document so that he could refer to it four weeks later in his own apostolic exhortation in order to give greater theological 'weight' to what he says there.

Francis maintains that at the present time those who adopt a gnostic position are people who imagine that what is really important is to have a correct *knowledge* of Church doctrine and Church law. These people desire to have 'a monolithic body of doctrine guarded by all and leaving no room for nuance' (*GE*, 43). They forget that Catholic teaching is not a closed system. Those who think they know the truth look down on the people they see as the 'ignorant masses'. They fail to realise that the questions, suffering, struggles, dreams, trials and worries of people 'all possess an interpretational value … their wondering helps us to wonder, their questions question us' (*GE*, 44).

On the other hand, present-day pelagians or semi-pelagians are people who, while taking account notionally of the need for grace, insist in practice that people can be expected by their own efforts of will to fully obey all the laws of the Church. These people have 'an obsession with the law' and 'a punctilious concern for the Church's liturgy' (*GE*, 57). They forget 'that everything "depends not on human will or exertion, but on God who shows mercy" (Rm 9:16) and that "he first loved us" (cf. 1 Jn 4:19)' (*GE*, 48).

Francis goes on to spell out the effects of such distorted spiritualities and theologies, and in doing so it is obvious that he is offering a defence of what he had to say about the possibility of divorced people receiving Holy Communion, in the controversial footnote to *Amoris Laetitia*. He says: 'Unless we can acknowledge our concrete and limited situation, we will not be able to see the real and possible steps that the Lord demands of us at every moment, once we are attracted and empowered by his gift … If we reject this historical and progressive reality, we can actually refuse and block grace, even as we extol it by our words' (*GE*, 50).

In fact what Francis is putting forward is a justification for his emphasis in all of his writings and addresses on the grace and mercy of God and on the importance of a gradualist approach – taking people 'where they are at' and not demanding more of them than they can do at the particular moment. He insists that 'in this life human weaknesses are not healed completely and once for all by grace' (*GE*, 49) and he backs this up with a footnote (48) in which he quotes a statement from St Thomas Aquinas which says that grace does not fully heal humans.

SAME-SEX MARRIAGE

We should not forget that *Amoris Laetitia* represents the response of Pope Francis to the dialogue and outcome of the two-session Synod of Bishops which he had established and which took place in 2014 and 2015. So the question arises whether his document has anything significant to say on the issue of same-sex marriage which had become a live issue around that time in much of the Western world, and which had been a concern for some of the bishops during the Synod.

Towards the end of the first session of the Synod in October 2014, the interim report had a section entitled 'Welcoming Homosexual Persons'. It said: 'Homosexuals have gifts and qualities to offer to the Christian community.' And it went on to ask, 'are we capable of welcoming these people, guaranteeing to them a fraternal space in our communities ... accepting and valuing their sexual orientation, without compromising Catholic doctrine on the family and matrimony?' (50) This provoked strong reaction both inside and outside the Synod; after much animated discussion among the participants, the final report of the 2014 session of the Synod omitted these statements. And in the following year, paragraph seventy-six of the final report of the 2015 session stated firmly: 'There are absolutely no grounds for considering homosexual unions to be in any way similar or even remotely analogous to God's plan for marriage and family. Nevertheless, men and women with a homosexual tendency ought to be received with respect and sensitivity.'

In the light of this strong statement from the Synod it is not surprising that in writing *Amoris Laetitia*, Francis did not include any of the controversial statements that had appeared in the 2014 interim report. He did not qualify in any way the official Catholic position that the Church does not accept that same-sex couples can get married. One might speculate that he would have wished to include some of the words from the interim report – for instance, some statement about welcoming homosexual people into the Christian community. But, true to his commitment to dialogue with the bishops, he simply quoted the words of the final report. He did, however, insist that 'families whose members include persons who experience same-sex attraction … should be given respectful pastoral guidance so that those who manifest a homosexual orientation can receive the assistance they need and fully carry out God's will in their lives.'

However, the strong focus in *Amoris Laetitia* on the subjective dimension of morality throws light on one of the more controversial remarks of Pope Francis. During his return flight from Brazil quite early in his pontificate, when asked about gay partnership, he had replied, 'who am I to judge?' His careful treatment in *Amoris Laetitia* of the difference between objective and subjective morality indicates that in his earlier remark he was not questioning the Catholic teaching that the practice of gay sex is objectively wrong; but he was not prepared to say that every homosexual act is invariably a mortal sin.

Chapter Three

'No' to Abortion, Death Penalty, and War

ABORTION

It had been suggested by some 'pro-life' campaigners that Francis is 'softer' than previous popes on the issue of abortion. So, in 2013, it brought some relief to those who set a very high priority to this issue to see his statement:

> Among the vulnerable for whom the Church wishes to care with particular love and concern are unborn children, the most defenceless and innocent among us ... This defence of unborn life is closely linked to the defence of each and every other human right. It involves the conviction that a human being is always sacred and inviolable, in any situation and at every stage of development. Human beings are ends in themselves and never a means of resolving other problems. (*EG*, 213)

On various occasions in subsequent years Francis made it very clear that he was strongly opposed to abortion and had no intention of weakening the Church's opposition to it. For instance, during an in-flight press conference on his way back from Mexico to Rome on 17 February 2016, Francis was asked by a reporter whether the Church would consider it as a 'lesser evil' to abort a baby in the womb who was infected with the

Zika virus. Francis replied, 'Abortion is not a "lesser evil". It is a crime. It is wiping out one to save another. ... It is a crime, it is absolutely evil ... It is an evil in and of itself.' Again, on 21 November 2016, following the closure of the Year of Mercy, during an interview with TV2000, Pope Francis called the practice of abortion a 'horrendous crime' and a 'very grave sin'.

Nevertheless, there are a significant number of conservative Catholics who continue to insist that Francis has softened the Church's position on this issue. It is clear that they want him to agree with their view that the abortion issue must have absolute priority. They were horrified when it was reported that in the Spadaro interview of 30 September 2013 he had said that the Church had become 'obsessed' with abortion, gay marriage and contraception, and that he had chosen not to talk about those issues despite recriminations from critics.

The reason why Francis does not agree with the view of those who believe that opposition to abortion must be given priority over all other moral issues is that he believes that the protection of human life and respect for it is a 'seamless garment' at every stage from womb to death. This view was expressed very clearly by him in a speech he gave on 30 May 2015, at a meeting of a science and life association:

> The plague of abortion is an attack on life. Allowing our brothers and sisters to die on boats in the strait in Sicily is an attack on life. Dying on the job because the minimum safety standards are not respected is an attack on life. Death from malnutrition is an attack on life. Terrorism, war, violence; so is euthanasia. Loving life means always taking

care of the other, wanting the best for him, cultivating and respecting her transcendent dignity.

Francis is well aware that some of those who campaign strongly against abortion are dissatisfied with his position. But he has refused to agree with them in adopting what is sometimes called 'a single issue' attitude. In *Gaudete et Exsultate* he has strongly reaffirmed his belief in the 'seamless garment' approach:

> Our defence of the innocent unborn … needs to be clear, firm and passionate, for at stake is the dignity of a human life, which is always sacred and demands love for each person, regardless of his or her stage of development. Equally sacred, however, are the lives of the poor, those already born, the destitute, the abandoned and the underprivileged, the vulnerable infirm and elderly exposed to covert euthanasia, the victims of human trafficking, new forms of slavery, and every form of rejection. We cannot uphold an ideal of holiness that would ignore injustice in a world where some revel, spend with abandon and live only for the latest consumer goods, even as others look on from afar, living their entire lives in abject poverty …
>
> Some Catholics consider it a secondary issue compared to the 'grave' bioethical questions. That a politician looking for votes might say such a thing is understandable, but not a Christian, for whom the only proper attitude is to stand in the shoes of those brothers and sisters of ours who risk their lives to offer a future to their children. Can we not realise that this is exactly what Jesus demands of us, when

he tells us that in welcoming the stranger we welcome him
(cf. Mt 25:35)? (*GE*, 101–2)

Francis added a footnote (84) in which he quotes from the 2007
Latin American *Aparecida Document* which states that 'life must
be safeguarded "starting at conception, *in all its stages*, until
natural death".'

CAPITAL PUNISHMENT

The opposition of Francis to capital punishment is another
example of his commitment to the 'seamless garment' position.

On 3 May 2014, Francis wrote an interesting letter to the
participants in the nineteenth conference of the International
Association of Penal Law. In his letter he said that 'an eye for an
eye or a tooth for a tooth … is no longer the proper response
to injury'. Then he added: 'Justice is not to be rendered to the
victim, by executing the aggressor.' In this way he made his
objection to capital punishment clear.

Just a few months later, on 23 October 2014, Francis gave a
remarkably forceful speech to the delegates of the International
Association of Penal Law. In it he protested strongly against the
modern tendency to look for scapegoats for problems in society:

Scapegoats are not only sought to pay, with their freedom
and with their lives, for all social ills such as was typical
in primitive societies, but over and beyond this, there is
at times a tendency to deliberately fabricate enemies:
stereotyped figures who represent all the characteristics
that society perceives or interprets as threatening. The

mechanisms that form these images are the same that allowed the spread of racist ideas in their time.

These remarks of Francis about scapegoating have clearly been influenced by the ground-breaking studies by René Girard on this topic (cf. Girard 1989).

In this speech, Francis went on to take a strong stance against the use of the death penalty:

> There are many well-known arguments against the death penalty. The Church has duly highlighted several, such as the possibility of judicial error and the use made by totalitarian and dictatorial regimes who use it as a means of suppressing political dissidence or of persecuting religious and cultural minorities.

He stated that at the present time it is 'impossible to imagine that States' have no other way of protecting people from unjust aggressors than to resort to capital punishment. So he concluded that 'all Christians and people of good will are thus called today to fight ... for the abolition of the death penalty, whether legal or illegal, and in all its forms.'

Francis even went so far as to condemn life imprisonment, saying: 'A life sentence is just a death penalty in disguise.' Furthermore, he said that Christians and people of good will are called to fight for the improvement of prison conditions, out of respect for the human dignity of the people who have been deprived of their freedom. And he uttered a quite detailed condemnation of all kinds of torture and of political corruption.

In a letter of 20 March 2015 to the President of the International Commission against the Death Penalty, Francis again came out strongly against the use of capital punishment. He pointed out that, relying on scripture and tradition, the Church authorities have for millennia defended human life from conception to natural death, teaching that human life is sacred because, from the first moment of conception, it is the fruit of the creative action of God. He went on to say that 'not even a murderer loses his personal dignity, and God himself pledges to guarantee this'. Francis then made this solemn declaration:

> Today capital punishment is unacceptable, however serious the condemned's crime may have been. It is an offence to the inviolability of life and to the dignity of the human person which contradicts God's plan for humans and for society and his merciful justice, and it fails to conform to any just purpose of punishment. It does not render justice to the victims, but rather foments revenge.

The Pope then went on to claim that the death penalty loses all legitimacy because of the possibility of judicial error and because of 'the defective selectivity of the criminal justice system'. He said:

> Human justice is imperfect, and the failure to recognise its fallibility can transform it into a source of injustice. With the application of capital punishment, the person sentenced is denied the possibility to make amends or to repent of the harm done; the possibility of confession, with which the person expresses inner conversion; and of contrition, the

means of repentance and atonement, in order to reach the encounter with the merciful and healing love of God.

He went on to say that capital punishment is a frequent practice to which totalitarian regimes and fanatical groups resort, for the extermination of political dissidents, minorities, and every individual labelled as 'dangerous' or who might be perceived as a threat to their power or to the attainment of their objectives. As in the first centuries and also in the current one, the Church suffers from the application of this penalty to her new martyrs.

Francis added that the death penalty entails cruel, inhumane and degrading treatment. He claimed that the anguish before the moment of execution and the terrible suspense between the issuing of the sentence and the execution of the penalty, are a form of 'torture'. And this 'torture' may well last for many years, and often leads to illness and insanity on death row. In regard to the debate about the 'best' method of execution, Francis says simply, 'There is no humane form of killing another person.'

Towards the end of his letter Francis notes that nowadays there is 'a heightened moral sensitivity regarding the value of human life'. This has the effect of arousing public opinion in support of the abolition of capital punishment, or at least ensuring that nobody is actually executed.

Finally, Francis puts forward a compelling case against sentences of life imprisonment, or other extremely long prison sentences. He says that these may be considered as 'hidden death sentences'. This is because they 'render it impossible for the condemned to plan a future in freedom'. With them 'the guilty party is not only deprived of his/her freedom, but insidiously deprived of hope'.

Francis maintains that the criminal justice system must never take away the hope of those who have been imprisoned.

CHANGE OR DEVELOPMENT?

Francis gave an address on 11 October 2017 to participants in the meeting promoted by the pontifical council for promoting the New Evangelisation. In this speech he repeated more strongly than ever his condemnation of the death penalty. But he also added a new dimension to this teaching by explaining in some detail that this is not a *change* in the Church's doctrine but rather an authentic development. He began by saying that the *Catechism of the Catholic Church* needs to be adapted in order to provide 'a more adequate and coherent treatment' on this topic. He said:

> It must be clearly stated that the death penalty is an inhumane measure that, regardless of how it is carried out, abases human dignity. It is *per se* contrary to the Gospel, because it entails the wilful suppression of a human life that never ceases to be sacred in the eyes of its Creator and of which – ultimately – only God is the true judge and guarantor … the death penalty is inadmissible because it is an attack on the inviolability and the dignity of the person.

Francis went on to explain why he felt it necessary to take a stronger and clearer position than had been taken by previous popes and by the Catholic Catechism. He noted that in past centuries, when means of defence were scarce and when society was less developed and mature, justice seemed to require the use of the death penalty. He maintained, however, that even at that time the imposition of the death penalty 'was dictated by a mentality more legalistic than Christian'. He added that nowadays, when we have a stronger sense of the call to protect human dignity, we would be even more guilty if we were to claim that capital punishment is still needed.

On this occasion Francis was not content to speak out strongly and unequivocally against capital punishment. He also put up a strong defence against those who claimed that he was not entitled to 'change' Catholic doctrine in this way. He said: 'Here we are not in any way contradicting past teaching, for the defence of the dignity of human life from the first moment of conception to natural death has been taught by the Church consistently and authoritatively.' To those who disagreed with this claim, he responded by saying that 'the harmonious development of doctrine demands that we cease to defend arguments that now appear clearly contrary to the new understanding of Christian truth'. Invoking the ancient teaching of St Vincent of Lérins, Francis said boldly:

Tradition is a living reality and only a partial vision regards the 'deposit of faith' as something static. The word of God cannot be moth-balled like some old blanket in an attempt to keep insects at bay! No. The word of God is a dynamic and living reality that develops and grows because it is aimed at a fulfilment that none can halt. This law of progress … is a distinguishing mark of revealed truth as it is handed down by the Church, and in no way represents a change in doctrine.

This clear and forceful account of the difference between a *development* of doctrine and a *change* of doctrine is the response of Francis to those who questioned his authoritative teaching about capital punishment. We may, however, suspect that in doing so he was also responding subtly and indirectly to the vociferous critics who questioned what he had said in *Amoris Laetitia* about the contentious issue of the reception of the Holy Communion by some people who had been divorced and remarried.

NON-VIOLENCE RATHER THAN 'JUST WAR'

In recent years a significant number of theologians have begun to call into question the traditional 'just war' teaching of the Catholic Church. They hold firstly that the nature of modern warfare means that it is impossible in practice to fulfil the conditions for waging such a war. And secondly they believe that alternatives such as the use of sanctions made war unnecessary.

From 11–13 April 2016, an important three-day conference was held in Rome and co-hosted by the Pontifical Council for Justice and Peace and the international Catholic peace organisation, Pax Christi. It brought together eighty participants including bishops, theologians and peace campaigners from all over the world. The title of the conference was 'Non-violence and Just Peace: Contributing to the Catholic Understanding of and Commitment to Non-violence'. The participants were energised by a message of Pope Francis, in which he said that their 'thoughts on revitalising the tools of non-violence, and of active non-violence in particular, will be a needed and positive contribution'.

After an exciting and fruitful dialogue the participants issued a quite radical document entitled 'An Appeal to the Catholic

Church to Re-Commit to the Centrality of Gospel Non-violence'. A key passage in the document was:

> We believe that there is no 'just war'. Too often the 'just war theory' has been used to endorse rather than prevent or limit war. Suggesting that a 'just war' is possible also undermines the moral imperative to develop tools and capacities for nonviolent transformation of conflict. We need a new framework that is consistent with Gospel non-violence.

So they went on to say: 'We propose that the Catholic Church develop and consider shifting to a 'just peace' approach based on Gospel non-violence. A 'just peace' approach offers a vision and an ethic to build peace as well as to prevent, defuse, and to heal the damage of violent conflict.' Then they called on Pope Francis 'to share with the world an encyclical on non-violence and just peace'. And they committed themselves to furthering Catholic understanding and practice of active non-violence – and not to use or teach 'just war theory' any longer.

It is against this background that Pope Francis issued his 2017 Message for the Fiftieth World Day of Peace. This document was issued on 8 December 2016, under the title 'Non-violence: a Style of Politics for Peace'. In it, Francis made a passionate appeal for the rejection of war and for peace-building through *active non-violence*. In paragraph three he said: '[Jesus] taught his disciples to love their enemies … Jesus marked out the path of non-violence … To be true followers of Jesus today also includes embracing his teaching about non-violence.'

In the following paragraph he pointed out that non-violence does not mean passive surrender. And he went on to recall the 'impressive results' of people like Gandhi, Martin Luther King, and 'the thousands of Liberian women, who organised pray-ins and nonviolent protest that resulted in high-level peace talks to end the second civil war in Liberia'. He noted that 'efforts on behalf of the victims of injustice and violence are not the legacy of the Catholic Church alone, but are typical of many religious traditions'. Then he said: 'Let us never tire of repeating: "The name of God cannot be used to justify violence."'

In paragraph five he pleaded for disarmament and for the prohibition and abolition of nuclear weapons, protesting against the concept of nuclear deterrence. Towards the end of the document he made a solemn commitment: 'I pledge the assistance of the Church in every effort to build peace through active and creative non-violence.'

NUCLEAR WEAPONS

Pope Francis was not content to make this strong plea. He decided to take a more radical step, one which involves a major change in Catholic social teaching, in regard to nuclear weapons. It concerns the official stance of the Catholic Church on the issue of the possession and use of nuclear weapons. Thirty-five years earlier, Pope John Paul II had called for the abolition of these weapons. But in paragraph eight of his message to the United Nations on 7 June 1982, he had said: 'In current conditions "deterrence" based on balance, certainly not as an end in itself but as a step on the way toward a progressive disarmament, may still be judged morally acceptable.' So he was saying that the *possession* of nuclear bombs could be acceptable in the Cold War situation of that time, even though the use of these weapons would be morally wrong.

In a speech on 10 November 2017, Francis went much further than any of his predecessors. He bluntly condemned even the *possession* of such weapons and the threat to use them. He was addressing the participants in an international symposium entitled, 'Prospects for a World Free of Nuclear Weapons and for Integral Disarmament'. He said that we cannot fail 'to be genuinely concerned by the catastrophic humanitarian and environmental effects of any employment of nuclear devices'. Then he went on to say:

> If we also take into account the risk of an accidental detonation as a result of error of any kind, *the threat of their use, as well as their very possession, is to be firmly condemned.* For they exist in the service of a mentality of fear that affects not only the parties in conflict but the entire human race. International relations cannot be held captive to military force, mutual intimidation, and the parading of stockpiles of arms. Weapons of mass destruction, particularly nuclear weapons, create nothing but a false sense of security. They cannot constitute the basis for peaceful coexistence between members of the human family, which must rather be inspired by an ethics of solidarity. (emphasis added)

Francis added that 'weapons that result in the destruction of the human race are senseless even from a tactical standpoint'. He went on to remind his audience of the historic vote at the United Nations where a large majority of states declared that nuclear weapons are *immoral* and must also be considered an *illegal* means of warfare. Francis noted the important fact that this 'humanitarian initiative' was 'sponsored by a significant alliance between civil society, states, international organisations, churches, academies and groups of experts'. (Sadly, we must note that the states which actually possess nuclear weapons resisted this initiative and refused to accept it.)

In the course of his press conference during his flight back to Rome from Bangladesh on 2 December 2017, Francis was asked what had changed between the present and the time in 1982 when John Paul II had allowed that nuclear weapons could be held as a deterrent under some conditions. Suggesting that there is even greater irrationality at the present time, he said that there is now such a sophisticated arsenal of nuclear weapons that there is a risk that the whole human race – or at least a large part of it – may be destroyed. And he added that we have reached the limit of what is morally acceptable so it is time to step back.

CONCLUSION

When we put together the teaching of Pope Francis on the issues of abortion, capital punishment, nuclear weapons, and non-violence it is clear that he is committed to promoting a fully consistent-ethics-of-life approach which embraces all of these elements. In fact, as I shall suggest in a later chapter, his defence-of-life commitment extends not only to all aspects of human life but also to other living creatures with whom we humans share this planet.

Chapter Four

Structural Injustice

THE CRY OF THE POOR

One of the most frequent challenges posed by Francis to Christians everywhere, and to their pastors, is to 'hear the cry of the poor' (*EG,* 191). He insists that his dream is of something much more than simply providing poor people with what he calls a 'dignified sustenance'. Those who are poor need 'education, access to health care, and above all employment, for it is through free, creative, participatory and mutually supportive labour that human beings express and enhance the dignity of their lives'. And he goes on at once to emphasise the importance of a just wage, for it is only in this way that they can have 'adequate access to all the other goods which are destined for our common use' (*EG,* 192).

Francis gave an important address at FAO (Food and Agriculture Organization of the United Nations) in Rome on World Food Day 16 October 2017. He said:

> I ask myself – and I ask you – this question: is it too much to consider introducing into the language of international cooperation the category of love, understood as gratuitousness, equal treatment, solidarity, the culture of giving, fraternity, mercy? Indeed these words express the practical content of the term 'humanitarian', widely used in international activities.

Francis was realistic enough to know that in some of the wealthier countries there are politicians, economists, and commentators who deny or play down the need for radical change of structures on behalf of those who are poor or excluded. He knew also that a significant number of those who hold this view are Catholics, and that some of them are Church leaders and commentators who claim that their position is fully in line with Catholic social teaching. So one must assume that he has these people in mind when he says: 'This message is so clear and direct, so simple and eloquent, that no ecclesial interpretation has the right to relativise it' (*EG,* 194).

Francis had a lengthy dialogue on 19 November 2013 with the leaders of the religious congregations of men. As reported by Fr Antonio Spadaro, the Pope referred to a letter that had been written years ago by Fr Pedro Arrupe, former general of the Jesuits, a letter in which Arrupe had referred to the necessity for some real contact with the poor. According to Spadaro's account, the Pope then said: 'This is really important to me: the need to become acquainted with reality by experience, to spend time walking on the periphery in order to really become acquainted with the reality and life experience of people' (Dialogue with leaders of USG).

CONDEMNATION OF PRESENT-DAY CAPITALISM

In the social and political sphere the most controversial element in the new approach of Pope Francis is his extraordinarily blunt condemnation of the present world order, where there is an ever-widening gap between rich and poor:

While the earnings of a minority are growing exponentially, so too is the gap separating the majority from the prosperity enjoyed by those happy few. (*EG, 56*)

He goes on immediately to point out that this is no accident:

This imbalance is the result of ideologies which defend the absolute autonomy of the marketplace and financial speculation … A new tyranny is thus born, invisible and often virtual, which unilaterally and relentlessly imposes its own laws and rules. (*EG, 56*)

Of course, the condemnation of an unregulated capitalist system has been a basic part of Catholic social teaching over the past one hundred and thirty years. But what is new is the freshness and harshness of Francis' words and the vividness with which he spells out the consequences of the present-day dominant ideology. In the first paragraph of his Message for World Day of Peace 2014, he says:

New ideologies, characterised by rampant individualism, egocentrism and materialistic consumerism, weaken social bonds, fuelling that 'throw away' mentality which leads to contempt for, and the abandonment of, the weakest and those considered 'useless'.

In *Evangelii Gaudium* he uses even stronger words: 'Human beings are themselves considered consumer goods to be used and then discarded. We have created a "throw away" culture which is now spreading. It is no longer simply about exploitation and oppression, but something new ... The excluded are not the "exploited" but the outcast, the "leftovers"' (*EG*, 53). In his October 2014 address to activists he spells this out more fully: 'The excluded are discarded as "leftovers" ... This is what takes place when the god of money is at the centre of an economic system ... Children are disposed of ... because ... neither children nor the elderly are producers' (*Movements*).

In the light of this outspoken condemnation of the capitalist system as it is practised at present, it is no wonder that the conservative radio host Rush Limbaugh should say about *Evangelii Gaudium*: 'This is just pure Marxism coming out of the mouth of the Pope.' Apparently the direct and uncompromising quality of Francis' words is more effective than the measured statements of previous popes in making it clear that the present political-economic system is quite incompatible with Catholic social teaching.

CHANGE IN THE STRUCTURES

Francis is not content just to condemn the evils of the system or to appeal to those in power to change their attitudes and approach. Nor is he content merely to advocate welfare programmes to help the poor survive. Instead, he calls loudly for governments and society to bring about changes in the political-economic structures: 'Welfare projects, which meet certain urgent needs, should be considered merely temporary responses' (*EG*, 202).

He goes to the root of the problem when he says: 'As long as the problems of the poor are not radically resolved by rejecting the absolute autonomy of markets and financial speculation and by attacking the structural causes of inequality, no solution will be found for the world's problems or, for that matter, to any problems' (*EG*, 202). He even goes so far as to say that 'the socioeconomic system is unjust at its root' (*EG*, 59). That is why he calls for a radical change in the very structure of the economic system.

In his insistence on the need for structural change, Francis is adopting one of the main themes of liberation theology. This means that his response to this theology is significantly different from that of Benedict XVI, whose suspicion of this theology led him to adopt what would be called a 'moralising' approach – that is, an emphasis more on personal conversion than on structural transformation.

Of course, Francis is not so naïve as to believe that structural changes can be a substitute for radical personal change. In fact, he insists on the need for an attitudinal and cultural transformation alongside a change in political and economic structures: 'Changing structures without generating new convictions and attitudes will only ensure that those same structures will become, sooner or later, corrupt, oppressive and ineffectual' (*EG*, 189).

This change of convictions and attitudes must lead to a change in lifestyle by those of us who are relatively well off. So Francis stresses the fundamental need for 'the detachment of those who choose to live a sober and essential lifestyle, of those who, by sharing their own wealth, thus manage to experience fraternal communion with others' (Peace Message 2014).

JUSTICE AND CHARITY
Popes are invariably too diplomatic to overtly reject a teaching espoused by an immediate predecessor. However, it appears that

on one major issue Pope Francis has adopted a position that is distinctly different, at least in emphasis, from that of Benedict XVI. That issue is the Church's stance in relation to charity and justice – an issue which has important practical implications.

In his first encyclical *Deus Caritas Est*, Pope Benedict had insisted that the official Church has only an indirect involvement in the promotion of justice in the world but that charity is a direct and essential element in the life of the Church. He seemed to be proposing that official Catholic relief and development agencies should concentrate particularly on giving immediate charitable relief in emergency situations, rather than supporting people's struggles for justice and long-term human development. Furthermore, he mandated the Vatican agency 'Cor Unum' to exercise effective control over 'Caritas Internationalis', which is a network of one hundred and sixty-four Caritas agencies in practically every country in the world.

This downgrading of Caritas Internationalis would mean that this decentralised and participatory network would now be under the direct control of a highly conservative agency in the Roman curia. This would seriously undermine the ethos and daily practice of the on-the-ground Catholic development agencies all over the world.

Pope Francis did not explicitly repudiate this initiative of his predecessor. But it is significant that Cardinal Oscar Andrés Rodríguez Maradiaga, who was at that time the president of Caritas Internationalis, was the person Francis chose as the chair of his body of eight cardinal advisers. And it was hardly a coincidence that the Pope himself, in a video on 10 December 2013, gave his explicit support to the launch of a major appeal by Caritas Internationalis: 'I give all my support to the Caritas Internationalis campaign against world hunger ... We are facing a global scandal where nearly a billion people go hungry. We cannot turn the other way and pretend it does not exist.' What is particularly notable is that the appeal to which the Pope was giving his support included the following words of Cardinal Maradiaga:

> The work of Caritas organisations on hunger ranges from providing food aid in times of crisis to longer-term programmes improving small-scale agriculture, livestock breeding, infrastructure, agro-forestry and reforestation. Caritas also promotes civic participation on social and economic issues such as access to markets, nutrition, water and sanitation for vulnerable communities.

This means that Pope Francis was giving his strong support to Caritas programmes concerned not just with emergency aid but with long-term human development.

The whole approach of Francis indicated that he had reverted to the traditional theology so well expressed by St Thomas Aquinas when he said, 'Charity [or love] is the form of all the virtues.' What this means in practice is that it is a mistake to oppose charity to justice, since action in support of justice is itself a form of charity, taking the word 'charity' in its broad sense. Providing charitable relief is, of course, one way in which individual Christians and the official Church respond to the call to put their love into action; but so too are action on behalf of justice and long-term human development, defence of human rights, work to promote reconciliation, and action to care for the environment. The statements and documents of Francis give no indication that he believes that charitable relief is more central or important than any of these other activities in the life of the Church and of Christians.

While Francis puts a lot of emphasis on structural injustice he also speaks out strongly against specific cases of injustice. One striking instance is his very blunt condemnation of the outrageous treatment of the Yazidi people in Iraq by ISIS, the so-called Islamic State. On 24 January 2018, when meeting a group of Yazidis who had come to live in Germany, he said: 'I raise my voice in defence of the rights of the Yazidis … no one can claim the power to wipe out a religious group on the grounds that they are not part of those whom they consider may be "tolerated".'

Chapter Five

Francis as a Liberation Activist

Already in *Evangelii Gaudium*, Francis had wholeheartedly adopted a key element of liberation theology: that making an option for the poor is not a one-way process. Francis maintains that we as Christians 'need to let ourselves be evangelised by them'. He spells this out, insisting that we are invited 'to acknowledge the saving power at work in their lives ... to find Christ in them, to lend our voice to their causes, but also to be their friends, to listen to them, to speak for them and to embrace the mysterious wisdom which God wishes to share with us through them' (*EG*, 198). Earlier in that document he maintains that the various examples of the 'popular piety' of poor people are the work of the Holy Spirit and a *locus theologicus* – the means used by God to share with us that divine 'mysterious wisdom' (*EG*, 126).

Although Pope Francis adopted several key elements in liberation theology in *Evangelii Gaudium*, he did explicitly emphasise one important element of this theology. That is the need for empowered poor people to challenge the rich and the powerful. However, eleven months later, on 28 October 2014, Francis gave a major address to a large group of social activists who had come to Rome from several different countries. They were representatives of the so-called 'popular movements'.[1] In this address he made it quite clear that he fully accepted the need for such activists to support poor people in the struggle for justice against the rich and the powerful. The whole tone of his words on that occasion is that of a person who identifies with these activists as his colleagues and friends.

He told them: 'You have your feet in the mud, you ... carry the smell of your neighbourhood, your people, your struggle! We want your voices to be heard – voices that are rarely heard. No doubt this is because ... your cries are bothersome, no doubt because people are afraid of the change that you seek' (*Movements*). His use, with obvious approval, of the word 'struggle' is quite striking; it represents a sharp departure from the almost invariant stance of previous popes. It is a clear indication that Francis had adopted the significant and most controversial feature of liberation theology.

He begins by saying that their presence is a sign or witness to a reality that is often silenced, namely, that 'the poor do not only suffer injustice; they also struggle against it!' Speaking directly to these activists, he said:

You are not satisfied with empty promises, with alibis or excuses. Nor do you wait with arms crossed for NGOs to help, for welfare schemes or paternalistic solutions that

---

1 In the interest of brevity, in references to this speech I shall call it *Movements*. It is important to note that in this mainly Latin American context the word 'popular' does not mean 'widely liked' or 'widely accepted' as in English. Perhaps the nearest one could get to an accurate English translation of the term *movimientos populares* would be 'movements of the common people'. And in the so-called 'developing countries' where most of these movements are located, the 'common people' are in fact *poor* people.

never arrive; or if they do, then it is with a tendency to anaesthetise or to domesticate ... and this is rather perilous. One senses that the poor are no longer waiting. You want to be protagonists. You get organised, study, work, issue demands and, above all, practise that very special solidarity that exists among those who suffer, among the poor, and that our civilization seems to have forgotten or would strongly prefer to forget. (*Movements*)

Some of his words could well have been spoken by any of the pioneers of liberation theology: 'The scandal of poverty cannot be addressed by promoting strategies of containment that only tranquilise the poor and render them tame and inoffensive. How sad it is when we find, behind allegedly altruistic works, the other being reduced to passivity or being negated; or worse still, we find hidden personal agendas or commercial interests.' Francis makes it clear that he fully identifies with the ministry of these activists:

How marvellous it is ... when we see peoples moving forward, especially their young and their poorest members. Then one feels a promising breeze that revives hope for a better world. May this breeze become a cyclone of hope. This is my wish. (*Movements*)

These words suggest that Francis as pope is prepared to give effective support to on-the-ground activists and to Church leaders who remain close to poor people in a committed and risky but nonviolent struggle for justice. This would represent a distinct break from the attitude of Pope John Paul II during most of his papacy, that is, once the Polish activists had succeeded in toppling the communist regime. Some of John Paul's warnings and most of the practical policies of the Vatican during this period gave the clear impression that the more liberation-minded activists and Church leaders had gone too far and that Rome actively disapproved of them.

In his passionate address to these activists, Francis delivered what one might almost call a diatribe against a whole list of abuses, which for him are an intrinsic aspect of the present unjust order. He mentioned the hoarding of land, deforestation, privatisation of the water supply, and the use of dangerous pesticides. Then he pointed out that millions of people die when the price of food is determined by financial speculation while tonnes of food are thrown away: 'Hunger is criminal, food is an inalienable human right.'

Francis went on to speak out strongly against homelessness and against the euphemisms that are employed to disguise the crimes committed in the whole area of housing. He expressed his outrage about the manner in which settlements of poor people are marginalised or even wiped out, as bulldozers are brought in to flatten the shacks of the poor. The proper alternative, he insisted, is a genuine and respectful urban integration where every neighbourhood is a real community. In such communities the people would have security of tenure and the area would have adequate amenities such as schools, health centres and sports clubs.

Next, Pope Francis spoke with equal passion about abuses in relation to work. He insisted that the worst form of poverty and indignity is the creation of a situation where people cannot find work. He maintained that it is by no means inevitable that young people should suffer unemployment. It is not necessary that people be forced to work in what is euphemistically called 'the informal sector'. Furthermore, there is no need for people to be deprived of basic labour rights. These injustices, he insisted, are the result of the deliberate prior decision by those in power to opt for a system that gives priority to profit rather than to human beings. They are the marks of a throwaway culture that treats humans as 'a consumer good, which can be used and then thrown away'. Later in his address he spoke of 'the balance sheets of economies that sacrifice people at the feet of the idol of money'.

Alongside his sharp condemnation, Pope Francis made clear his support both for those who are victims of abuses and for the activists who are working to change the system. He warmly praised those 'excluded workers, the discards of this system' who have succeeded in inventing work, using 'materials that seemed to be devoid of further productive value' in a people's economy through their solidarity and their community work. Waxing lyrical, Francis said that this is not just work, 'this is poetry!'

Then he spoke of the rights of 'every worker, within the formal system of salaried employment or outside it'. He listed all kinds of workers, mentioning the waste collectors, recyclers, peddlers, seamstresses and tailors, street traders, fishermen, farmworkers, builders, miners, workers in previously abandoned enterprises, members of cooperatives, and all kinds of workers in grassroots jobs who are denied workers' rights and the opportunity to join trade unions, and who do not have a steady or adequate income. He insisted that all of these have the right to decent remuneration for their work and also to social security and to a retirement pension. He said: 'I want today to join my voice to yours and to support you in your struggle.'

He told the activists to whom he was speaking that the movements they represent are expressions of 'the urgent need to revitalise our democracies'. For him it is a matter of 'active participation of great majorities as protagonists'. This kind of 'proactive participation overflows the logical procedures of formal democracy':

> Moving towards a world of lasting peace and justice calls us to go beyond paternalistic forms of assistance; it calls us to create new forms of participation that include popular movements and invigorate local, national and international governing structures with that torrent of moral energy that springs from including the excluded in the building of a common destiny. And all this with a constructive spirit, without resentment, with love.

It involves the establishment of genuine solidarity: 'Solidarity … means fighting against the structural causes of poverty and inequality, of the lack of work, land and housing; and of the denial of social and labour rights … Solidarity, understood in its deepest sense, is a way of making history.' This, he said, is what the people's movements are doing.

It is true, of course, that as Gerry O'Hanlon rightly reminds us that 'not everything that the Pope says is to be taken as carrying equal weight' (O'Hanlon 2015, 29). So the words of

Francis in this speech do not have the same formal authority as the words of an encyclical. Nevertheless, this address was not just an informal and spontaneous set of remarks but was clearly part of the Pope's formal teaching and was treated as such on the Vatican website. The address must be seen as a clear indication of the Pope's strongly held belief in the need for radical initiatives and struggle by social activists.

In the light of his quite radical remarks we can see why Francis said to these activists: 'It is strange but, if I talk about this, some say that the Pope is communist.' Rejecting this accusation strongly, he insisted that love for the poor is a central element of the Gospel, that the things the activists are struggling for – land, housing, and work – are sacred rights, and that there is nothing unusual about making this claim, since it is simply part of the social teaching of the Church (cf. *Movements*).

A SECOND MEETING WITH ACTIVISTS

In July 2015, Pope Francis embarked on a visit to three Latin American countries, during which time he made some important speeches that reinforced the message of his encyclical *Laudato Si'* and located it within a wider context. Particularly important was his very radical address on 9 July, in the city of Santa Cruz de la Sierra in Bolivia, to a gathering of social activists, members of 'popular movements' from several countries.

Speaking to this group, he warmly recalled his previous meeting with them several months earlier in Rome. At this second meeting he was even more explicit in condemning exploitation and encouraging those who struggle against it. Being fully aware that many of the more conservative bishops in Latin America offer little support to these Church activists, Francis diplomatically challenged their approach. He said:

> I am pleased to see the Church opening her doors to all of you, embracing you, accompanying you and establishing in each diocese, in every justice and peace commission, a genuine, ongoing and serious cooperation with popular movements. I ask everyone, bishops, priests and laity, as well as the social organisations of the urban and rural peripheries, to deepen this encounter.

He then said: 'I wish to join my voice to yours in calling for the three "L's" for all our brothers and sisters: *land*, *lodging* and *labour*. I said it and I repeat it: these are sacred rights. It is important, it is well worth fighting for them.' Having mentioned some of the problems confronted by these people, he said:

> Let us not be afraid to say it: we want change, real change, structural change. This system is by now intolerable: farmworkers find it intolerable, labourers find it intolerable, communities find it intolerable, peoples find it intolerable … The earth itself – our sister, Mother Earth, as St Francis would say – also finds it intolerable.

Francis then went on to offer hope to these activists who are struggling to bring about change. He spoke of a change that is redemptive, and said that in his many meetings and travels he has 'sensed an expectation, a longing, a yearning for change, in people throughout the world'.

Speaking from the heart, he said: 'You, the lowly, the exploited, the poor and underprivileged, can do, and are doing, a lot. I would even say that the future of humanity is in great measure in your own hands, through your ability to organise and carry out creative alternatives.' He insisted that the seeds of hope are 'patiently sown in the forgotten fringes of our planet.' Later in his address he said:

> People and their movements are called to cry out, to mobilise and to demand – peacefully, but firmly – that appropriate and urgently needed measures be taken. I ask you, in the name of God, to defend Mother Earth ... The future of humanity does not lie solely in the hands of great leaders, the great powers and the elites. It is fundamentally in the hands of peoples and in their ability to organise.

Speaking of the importance of constructing 'a humane alternative to a globalisation which excludes', he said, 'The Church cannot and must not remain aloof from this process in her proclamation of the Gospel.' But then he went on to say:

> Don't expect a recipe from this pope. Neither the pope nor the Church has a monopoly on the interpretation of social reality or the proposal of solutions to contemporary issues. I dare say that no recipe exists. History is made by each generation as it follows in the footsteps of those preceding it, as it seeks its own path and respects the values which God has placed in the human heart.

Having insisted that the pope or the Church does not have a formula for a perfect society, Francis pointed out some relevant guiding principles:

> A just economy must create the conditions for everyone to be able to enjoy a childhood without want, to develop their talents when young, to work with full rights during their active years and to enjoy a dignified retirement as they grow older. It is an economy where human beings, in harmony with nature, structure the entire system of production and distribution in such a way that the abilities and needs of each individual find suitable expression in social life. You, and other peoples as well, sum up this desire in a simple and beautiful expression: 'to live well,' which is not the same as 'to have a good time.' Such an economy is not only desirable and necessary, but also possible. It is no utopia or chimera. It is an extremely realistic prospect. We can achieve it.

Francis repeated a point which had been made in 1991 by Pope John Paul II in his encyclical *Centesimus Annus* and which was misinterpreted by some right-wing Catholics as a rejection of any form of 'welfare state'. He said: 'Welfare programs geared to certain emergencies can only be considered temporary and incidental responses. They could never replace true inclusion, an inclusion which provides worthy, free, creative, participatory and solidary work.'

NEO-COLONIALISM

Francis goes on to appeal to 'my brothers and sisters of the popular movements' to work for unity between the different Latin American countries. He sees this as a way of resisting:

> the new colonialism [which] takes on different faces. At times it appears as ... certain 'free trade' treaties, and the imposition of measures of 'austerity' which always tighten the belt of workers and the poor ... Similarly, the monopolising of the communications media, which would impose alienating examples of consumerism and a certain cultural uniformity, is another one of the forms taken by the new colonialism. It is ideological colonialism ... colonialism, both old and new, which reduces poor countries to mere providers of raw material and cheap labour, engenders violence, poverty, forced migrations and all the evils which go hand in hand with these, precisely because, by placing the periphery at the service of the centre, it denies those countries the right to an integral development.

Towards the end of his address, Francis said, 'Some may rightly say, "When the Pope speaks of colonialism, he overlooks certain actions of the Church." I say this to you with regret: many grave sins were committed against the native peoples of America in the name of God ... I humbly ask forgiveness, not only for the offences of the Church herself, but also for crimes committed against the native peoples during the so-called conquest of America.'

Showing his sensitivity towards non-believers among his audience, Francis concluded his address by saying, 'I ask you, please, to pray for me. If some of you are unable to pray, with all respect, I ask you to send me your good thoughts and energy.'

This address of Pope Francis is a striking example of the unity of his vision: his concern for the environment and his concern for people who are poor and exploited are inextricably connected. Together, they are the basis for his passionate demand for a transformation of the present dominant mentality and policies – a radical conversion at the economic, political, cultural, and spiritual levels.

IN THE UNITED STATES

Many people wondered whether Francis would repeat his outspoken condemnation of the abuses of capitalism in the course of his visit to the United States. In fact, in his address to the joint session of the Congress on 24 September 2015, the tone of his remarks was quite different, and his overall approach was carefully calculated to appeal to his audience. Nevertheless, he succeeded in getting across the key points of his position. He shrewdly quoted a passage about business from his own encyclical in which he had pointed out that business must serve the common good:

> Business is a noble vocation, directed to producing wealth and improving the world. It can be a fruitful source of prosperity for the area in which it operates, especially if it sees the creation of jobs as an essential part of its service to the common good. (*LS*, 129)

Francis did not hesitate to use the controversial phrase 'unjust structures', pointing out, 'even in the developed world, the effects of unjust structures and actions are all too apparent'.

He went on to quote from the US Declaration of Independence, adding at once: 'If politics must truly be at the service of the human person, it follows that it cannot be a slave to the economy and finance.' Politics, he said, must serve the common good 'of a community which sacrifices particular interests in order to share, in justice and peace, its goods, its interests, its social life'.

In this way, Francis made it clear that he was not backing down from his condemnation of the type of unregulated capitalism which exploits people and the environment and thus fails to serve the common good. In a carefully nuanced passage he said: 'I would encourage you to keep in mind all those people around us who are trapped in a cycle of poverty. They too need to be given hope. The fight against poverty and hunger must be fought constantly and on many fronts, especially in its causes.' By emphasising the causes of poverty, he was diplomatically reminding the audience of his strong condemnation in his encyclical of '[the] deified market' (*LS*, 56).

Chapter Six

Inequality in Society and Relative Poverty

Economists and planners make a distinction between *absolute* poverty, where people lack the basic necessities of life, and *relative* poverty which refers to situations where there is a wide gap between the rich and those who are less well off. Pope Francis shows that he is well aware that Western politicians often defend the present economic order on the grounds that at least it has led to a reduction in the level of absolute poverty in most of the poorer countries. His response is unequivocal: 'If on the one hand we are seeing a reduction in absolute poverty, on the other hand we cannot fail to recognise that there is a serious rise in relative poverty, that is, instances of inequality between people and groups who live together in particular regions or in a determined historical-cultural context' (Peace Message 2014, 5). It is clear that he is calling for the elimination or major reduction in relative poverty as well as absolute poverty, for he says, 'Inequality is the root of social ills' (*EG,* 202).

There is scientific research which provides solid support for this statement of Pope Francis (cf. Wilkinson and Pickett 2010 passim; cf. Dorling 2014 passim). Furthermore, groundbreaking research by Thomas Piketty has shown how right Francis is to be concerned about the growth in relative poverty. Piketty's historical study puts forward a convincing case in favour of the view that throughout history the capitalist system has tended to widen the gap between the rich and the poor, except when this economic pattern has been broken by a political policy of having progressive taxes or by such exceptional events as major revolutions or wars. The basic reason for this, according to Piketty, is that, apart from exceptional situations, the share of income generated by capital has always tended to be greater than that which is earned by labour.

His detailed study documents the remarkable extent to which, particularly in the United States and Britain in the period between 1980 and the present, there has been a major reduction in the type of taxes which are designed to make society somewhat less unequal (e.g. Piketty 2014, 499, figure 14.1; 508–12). This change has given rise to an alarming widening of the gap between the very rich and the rest of the population.

Piketty's explanation of the widening gap between the rich and the poor was focused almost entirely on *economic* patterns. But I venture to add that one should also take account of the *political* reasons for the widening gap. Those who have economic power generally use their wealth both to influence politicians through lobbyists and to gain control of the media. In this way they ensure that political policies favour their interests and that large sections of the popular media fail to expose the close links between politicians and wealthy individuals or corporations.

Piketty holds that there are only two effective ways in which the widening gap between rich and poor can be bridged. The first is by the introduction of seriously 'progressive' taxation, that is, ensuring that the rate of taxation gets higher as people become more wealthy. The second way of reducing inequality would be to impose a global tax on capital or wealth (Piketty 2014, 512–13; 515–30; 572; 640 n. 51). He says that 'without a global tax on capital or some similar policy, there is a substantial risk that the top centile's share of global wealth will continue to grow indefinitely – and this should worry everyone' (519).

As one might have expected, Piketty's study stirred up a lot of controversy. Quite a number of conservative economists and commentators attacked his findings on various grounds, while many others rallied to his defence. Having examined a representative sample of this material, I have come to believe that, although the critics have located some relatively minor inadequacies in his study, on the whole Piketty's conclusions and proposals remain valid.

Far more detailed proposals for reducing inequality are spelled out by Anthony Atkinson. He puts forward fifteen key proposals which, if implemented, would have the effect of bringing about a radical reduction in the gap between the rich and the poor (Atkinson 2015 passim; summarised on pp. 303–4). His proposals include:

» a statutory minimum wage set at the level of a living wage;
» guaranteed public employment at the minimum wage for those who seek it;
» a progressive rate of income tax up to a top rate of 65 per cent;
» substantial child benefits.

Atkinson's study focuses mainly on the situation in the United States and Britain. Piketty expresses his regret that in Atkinson's study 'the space devoted to international matters is relatively limited' (Piketty 2015, 28).

The proposals put forward by Piketty and Atkinson could be implemented without seriously disrupting the effective economic workings of society at the national and international levels. In fact, these proposals or suggestions would greatly lessen the looming danger of a spiral that may lead to another major economic collapse in the world economy.

From the point of view of Catholic social teaching, perhaps the most valuable aspect of Piketty's and Atkinson's proposals are that they represent ways of realistically 'putting flesh on' demands by Pope Francis and other concerned people for structural change. Solidly grounded studies, such as those of Atkinson and Piketty, show that it is wrong to assume that the only alternative to the present unjust economic order is socialism. What these authors offer is a realistic way of restructuring the present free-market system without overthrowing it entirely. So their proposals may appeal to those who fear that Pope Francis' outspoken criticism of the present world order means that he is a communist or that he is in favour of a socialist system.

However, immensely powerful forces resist the kind of changes proposed by Piketty, Atkinson and many others. Very rich individuals and corporations have enormous power in both the political field and in the media. Furthermore, the present level of international cooperation in regard to taxes and the elimination of tax havens is grossly inadequate. It is for this reason that Piketty acknowledges: 'A global tax on capital is a utopian idea' (Piketty 2014, 515). Nevertheless, he goes on to say that 'it is perfectly possible to move towards this ideal solution step by step' (515).

This provides an incentive for Catholics to cooperate closely with other Christians, people of other religions, and all who are committed to working for justice in society to build a strong coalition that will campaign effectively for the necessary changes. In this, as on several other apparently unrealistic aspects of Catholic social teaching, we must 'hope against hope', holding on to our belief that sustained human commitment, fortified by divine grace, can bring about what had seemed virtually impossible.

Chapter Seven

Migration and Trafficking

The very first journey of Pope Francis outside of Rome was his trip on 8 July 2013 to the small island of Lampedusa where tens of thousands of migrants had landed after a dangerous sea-crossing. There he spoke from the heart about the immigrants who are 'dying at sea, in boats which were vehicles of hope and became vehicles of death':

> When I first heard of this tragedy a few weeks ago, and realised that it happens all too frequently, it has constantly come back to me like a painful thorn in my heart. So I felt that I had to come here today, to pray and to offer a sign of my closeness, but also to challenge our consciences lest this tragedy be repeated.

He went on to say:

> These brothers and sisters of ours were trying to escape difficult situations to find some serenity and peace; they were looking for a better place for themselves and their families, but instead they found death. How often do such people fail to find understanding, fail to find acceptance, fail to find solidarity. And their cry rises up to God!

On 17 February 2016, as a key part of his visit to Mexico, Francis travelled to Ciudad Juárez on the frontier with the USA. In his homily he spoke passionately about the plight of the 'thousands of immigrants from Central America and other countries, not forgetting the many Mexicans who also seek to pass over "to the other side".' He pointed out that it is 'a journey laden with grave injustices … a web that ensnares and always destroys the poorest.' The migrants, he said, endure all forms of violence. This applies especially to women and also to the young who are treated 'as "cannon fodder", persecuted and threatened when they try to flee the spiral of violence and the hell of drugs'.

Francis flew back to Rome on the same day. During the flight he was asked about the campaign promise of then presidential candidate Donald Trump to build a wall along the border between the USA and Mexico. In reply, Francis said:

> A person who thinks only of building walls, wherever it may be, and not of building bridges, is not Christian. This is not in the Gospel. What you were asking me, who to vote for or not: I won't interfere. I only say: if a man says these things, he is not Christian.

Two months later, during the return flight to Rome from his visit to Lesbos, in April 2016, Francis was asked a question about whether Europe could continue to have open borders between the countries of the Schengen Agreement. In his response, Francis again spoke with some passion. Without mentioning names, he made it quite clear how strongly he disagreed with those who, like President Trump and some European leaders, respond to the refugee and migrant crisis by building walls or other barriers to keep migrants out:

> I have always said that building walls is not a solution … It resolves nothing. We must build bridges. But bridges are built intelligently, with dialogue, with integration. That is why I can understand a certain apprehension. But for a country to close its borders resolves nothing, because in the long run it harms its own people. Europe urgently needs to create policies of welcoming and integration, of growth, of employment, of economic reform … All these things are bridges that will lead us not to build walls.

REFUGEES AND 'ECONOMIC REFUGEES'

Another reporter immediately asked him why he did not distinguish between refugees in the strict sense, and people who were migrating in order to escape from hunger and poverty in their own countries. His answer was blunt: 'I said today in my speech: "some flee from war, others flee from hunger". Both of these are the effects of exploitation, also of the earth itself.'

When Francis was flying back from Sweden to Rome on 1 November 2016, he was again questioned about the distinction between those who are refugees in the strict sense and the so-called 'economic refugees'. He accepted that there is a clear distinction in law between refugees in the strict sense and other migrants who are not refugees in the legal sense. Countries have a legal duty to accept people who fit the legal definition of refugees. However, he showed that he would want the better-off countries to open their hearts, as far as possible, not only to refugees but also to other migrants, many of whom are so-called 'economic refugees'. At the same time he pointed out that it is not enough just to *accept* refugees; countries must also work hard to *integrate* them:

> We have to distinguish between migrants and refugees, right? Migrants must be treated according to certain rules because migrating is a right, albeit a right which is highly regulated. On the other hand, being a refugee is the result of situations of war, suffering, hunger, terrible situations, and the refugee's status calls for great attention, greater effort ... I think that ... those who govern ... also have to calculate how best to settle them, because refugees must not only be accepted, but also integrated.

During the course of his weekly audience on 8 February 2017, Pope Francis spoke of an appeal 'not to build walls but bridges'; and he went on to suggest that the building of a wall 'is not a Christian gesture'. Understandably, this was taken as a veiled reference to the commitment of President Trump to build a wall on the border between the USA and Mexico. However, it was probably also intended as a protest against the barriers erected against migrants on the borders of some European countries.

The Message of Pope Francis for the 104th World Day of Migrants and Refugees 2018, issued on 15 August 2017, offers by far the most detailed and developed account of the Pope's view about how we should respond to the migrant crisis. He recalls how he has repeatedly expressed his particular concern for the lamentable situation of many migrants and refugees who are fleeing from war, persecution, natural disasters and poverty. He maintains that this situation 'is undoubtedly a "sign of the times" which I have tried to interpret, with the help of the Holy Spirit'. He goes on to spell out the four elements which he sees as essential for the proper treatment of migrants: they must be *welcomed*, *protected*, *promoted*, and *integrated*:

> *Welcoming* means, above all, offering broader options for migrants and refugees to enter destination countries safely and legally ... The second verb – *protecting* – may be understood as a series of steps intended to defend the rights and dignity of migrants and refugees, independent of their legal status ... The universal right to a nationality should be recognised and duly certified for all children at birth. The statelessness which migrants and refugees sometimes fall into can easily be avoided with the adoption of nationality legislation that is in conformity with the fundamental principles of international law. Migratory status should not limit access to national healthcare and pension plans ... *Promoting* essentially means a determined effort to ensure that all migrants and refugees – as well as the communities which welcome them – are empowered to achieve their potential as human beings ... I encourage a determined effort to promote the social and professional inclusion of migrants and refugees, guaranteeing for all – including those seeking asylum – the possibility of employment, language instruction and active citizenship ... The final verb – *integrating* – concerns the opportunities for

intercultural enrichment brought about by the presence of migrants and refugees. Integration is not an assimilation that leads migrants to suppress or to forget their own cultural identity.

On 28 October 2017, Pope Francis gave an important speech at a conference in Rome organised by COMECE, the Commission of the Bishops' Conference of the European Union. On that occasion he spoke about the duty of politicians to ensure that migration is not an indiscriminate and unregulated process. But he also insisted that 'migrants must not neglect their own grave responsibility to learn, respect and assimilate the culture and traditions of the nations that welcome them'.

HUMAN TRAFFICKING

The concern of Francis for all migrants applies especially to those who are victims of human trafficking. The word 'trafficking' is being used at present in two different senses. Journalists frequently use it to refer to the smuggling of migrants from one country to another. The assumption here is that these migrants *willingly* enter boats or trucks in order to reach their desired location. However, 'trafficking in persons' (TIP) in its more strict legal sense refers to people who are *forced* or *deceived* by criminals into sexual slavery or forced labour, or whose organs are stolen.

Long before he became pope, Francis had been deeply concerned about the plight of people who have been trafficked in the strict legal sense. He knew the problem quite directly, having worked closely with those fighting against human trafficking when he was archbishop in Buenos Aires. Almost as soon as he became pope he gave a high priority to overcoming this form of exploitation. In two places in *Evangelii Gaudium* he put this modern version of slavery at the top of the list of social evils (cf. *EG*, 75, 211). One has the sense that he was speaking in the light of his own experience of personal contact with the victims of trafficking when he made an impassioned plea and challenge:

> Where is your brother or sister who is enslaved? ... Let us not look the other way. There is greater complicity than we think. The issue involves everyone! This infamous network of crime is now well established in our cities, and many people have blood on their hands as a result of their comfortable and silent complicity. (*EG*, 211)

In his speech in October 2014 to delegates of the International Association of Penal Law (which I have cited in chapter two), Francis issued an exceptionally strong and detailed condemnation of human trafficking:

> Enslaving people, human trafficking and war crimes are recognised as crimes against humanity, both by international law and by many national laws. It is a crime against humanity. And since it is not possible to commit so complex a crime as human trafficking without the complicity, by action or omission, of States, it is evident that, when efforts to prevent and combat this phenomenon are insufficient, we are again facing a crime against humanity.

Francis devoted almost the whole of his address to foreign diplomats on 12 December 2013 to the issue of trafficking. He said:

> There is one area I would like to consider with you which concerns me deeply and which currently threatens the dignity of persons, namely, human trafficking. Such trafficking is a true form of slavery, unfortunately more and more widespread, which concerns every country, even the most developed. It is a reality which affects the most vulnerable in society: women of all ages, children, the handicapped, the poorest, and those who come from broken families and from difficult situations in society.

He returned to this topic in his Peace Message 2014. In the first paragraph of that message he referred to 'the tragic phenomenon of human trafficking, in which the unscrupulous prey on the lives and the desperation of others'; and in paragraph eight he referred to 'the abomination of human trafficking'.

In August 2013 Francis asked the Pontifical Academies of Sciences and of the Social Sciences to convene a workshop to examine human trafficking and modern slavery. This gathering took place in the Vatican on 2–3 November 2013. It had originally been intended that it would include only scholars who had studied and written about this topic. But at the request of on-the-ground activists the invitation was extended to sixty 'observers' – people who had practical experience of ministering to victims of trafficking. These observers were allowed to participate actively in the conference, and it was acknowledged that this provided an enriching experience for all the participants.

The Pope showed a particular interest in what was going on at the conference, and afterwards he engaged in dialogue with the activists. One of the participants was Detective Inspector Kevin Hyland of the London Metropolitan Police. He described a new and more effective programme which had been put in place at Scotland Yard, one that enables the victims of trafficking to testify in court against the traffickers.

Just a few months later two further developments on the trafficking issue took place within less than a month of each other. The first of these was on 17 March 2014 at the Vatican, where representatives from several of the great world religions signed a 'revolutionary and unprecedented' agreement called the 'Global Freedom Network', stating: 'Modern slavery and human trafficking are crimes against humanity'; they committed themselves to working together to eradicate modern forms of slavery and human trafficking by 2020.

The second development was a conference at the Vatican on 9–10 April 2014, in which once again Kevin Hyland played a key role. This brought together police and law enforcement officers from various parts of the world, as well as social workers who were dealing with the victims of trafficking. The participants agreed to advance their international cooperation to combat the scourge of trafficking. The conference led to the establishment of the 'Santa Marta Group', which works to abolish human trafficking. This is a body comprising international law enforcement agencies, civil society organisations, non-governmental organisations and the Catholic Church. The group is sponsored by the Catholic

Bishops' Conference of England and Wales, in collaboration with the London Metropolitan Police. In his address to the participants as he launched the group, Pope Francis said:

> Human trafficking is an open wound on the body of contemporary society, a scourge upon the body of Christ. It is a crime against humanity. The very fact of our being here to combine our efforts means that we want our strategies and areas of expertise to be accompanied and reinforced by the mercy of the Gospel, by closeness to the men and women who are victims of this crime.

Just before his address to the participants, the Pope held a private meeting with four rescued victims of human trafficking, two from Eastern Europe and two from South America.

Following on from that gathering the Vatican has hosted further conferences on trafficking. For instance, as recently as 4–6 November 2017, the Pontifical Academy of Social Sciences held a workshop in the Vatican on the topic 'Assisting Victims in Human Trafficking: Best Practice in Resettlement, Legal Aid and Compensation'. As on previous occasions, this was not just an academic dialogue; it included moving accounts by people who had themselves been enslaved and trafficked.

At two points in his address to the General Assembly of the United Nations on 25 September 2015, Francis spoke out strongly against the evil of trafficking in persons. When speaking of the 'war' against the criminal trade in narcotics, he said: 'Drug trafficking is by its very nature accompanied by trafficking in persons.' Earlier in his address he had listed various 'baneful consequences … of social and economic exclusion', including 'human trafficking, the marketing of human organs and tissues, the sexual exploitation of boys and girls, slave labour, including prostitution'.

Towards the end of his press conference on 1 November 2016, during the flight back to Rome from his visit to Sweden, a German reporter put this questions to Francis: 'Your Holiness, a few days ago you met the Santa Marta Group, which is involved in combating modern slavery and human trafficking, issues which in my mind are very close to your heart, not only as pope, but even earlier in Buenos Aires, where you were involved in these areas. Why? Was there a particular experience, even a personal one?' Francis responded by recounting some of his long involvement in these issues:

In Buenos Aires, as a priest, I had long been troubled by … the fact that Christ continues to suffer, that Christ is continuously crucified in his weakest brothers and sisters. … Then, as bishop, in Buenos Aires we also undertook initiatives, also with groups of non-Catholics and non-believers, to combat slave labour, especially among the Latin-American migrants that continue to come to Argentina. Their passports are taken away and they are put to slave labour in the factories, but locked in. Once, one of these places caught fire and the children had been put on the roof; all of them died, along with others who were not able to escape … They were in fact slaves, and this made an impression on me. Trafficking in human persons. I also worked with two congregations of religious sisters who work with prostitutes, slaves to prostitution. Once a year, all these slaves of the system had a Mass in Plaza de la Constitución, one of the places where trains arrive, like Termini. There Mass was celebrated with everyone ... Here in Italy, many groups of volunteers are combatting forms of enslavement in the workplace and among women.

On 9 February 2018 Pope Francis had a further meeting with the Santa Marta Group. In the course of his short address to them he emphasised the need 'to raise awareness of the growing need to support victims of these crimes by accompanying them on a path of reintegration into society and the recovery of their human dignity'.

Under Francis, there has been an ongoing commitment from the Vatican to the raising of awareness of trafficking and its elimination. This offers us hope that the issue of human trafficking will remain a high priority in Catholic social teaching.

Chapter Eight

The Structures of the Church

From the point of view of everyday life, the overarching contribution of Francis is his renewed emphasis on all that Vatican II stood for. In the thirty years before Francis became pope, the Roman authorities had frequently invoked Vatican II but had in fact engaged in a consistent attempt to play down its originality. Indeed, in some respects they had acted quite contrary to the direction proposed by the council. Perhaps the most striking example of this was the ever-increasing centralisation of power in the Roman curia with the consequent undermining of the concept of episcopal collegiality. From the moment when he became pope, Francis repeatedly affirmed his commitment to the vision of Vatican II.

One area in which the contribution of Francis to Catholic social teaching on justice is most controversial and (hopefully) most effective in practice is in his commitment to applying that teaching to the Church itself. From the beginning of his papacy he was evidently determined to make an option for those who could be seen as the poor in relation to the institutional Church – that is, those who had been left in a disadvantaged or marginal position. These include laypeople vis-à-vis clergy, and bishops' conferences and diocesan bishops vis-à-vis Vatican curia officials. From the beginning, Francis began to put into practice the fundamental teaching on collegiality espoused by Vatican II.

In other words, he applied the principle of subsidiarity to the exercise of leadership and authority in the life of the Church.

It is significant that Francis quotes from the important document *Octogesima Adveniens* (*OA*), which Pope Paul VI had issued in 1971. The passage which Francis quotes is one in which Paul pointed to the variety of different situations faced by the Church in different parts of the world and said: 'In the face of such widely varying situations, it is difficult for us to utter a unified message and to put forward a solution which has universal validity ... It is up to the Christian communities to analyse with objectivity the situation which is proper to their own country' (*OA* 4, quoted by Francis in *EG*, 184).

In the intervening years the commitment of Paul VI to govern the Church in a collegial manner had been largely ignored by Pope John Paul II and by Pope Benedict XVI – and more particularly by the Vatican curia. Francis was now pledging to put collegiality into practice. One of the most important ways in which he proposed to take seriously the emphasis of Vatican II on collegiality was by enabling the Synod of Bishops to play the major role which had been envisaged by the council. This was shown by his calling of a two-phase synod, held in the autumn of 2014 and of 2015. It became even more evident by his insistence on the importance of genuine dialogue and even disagreement among the synod participants (e.g. his 'introductory remarks' to the Synod Fathers on 5 October 2015).

Prior to the time of Pope Francis, when people wished to invoke the principle of subsidiarity, they were told bluntly by the Roman authorities that the principle applied in civil and political society but not in the Church. Francis, on the other hand, says in *Evangelii Gaudium*: 'I am conscious of the need to promote a sound "decentralisation"' (*EG*, 16). Later in this manifesto he goes on to say, 'In the dialogue with our Orthodox brothers and sisters, we Catholics have the opportunity to learn more about the meaning of episcopal collegiality and their experience of synodality' (*EG*, 246). He even goes so far as to make statements that must have seemed quite shocking to many in the Vatican:

> Since I am called to put into practice what I ask of others, I too must think about a conversion of the papacy ... The papacy and the central structures of the universal Church also need to hear the call to pastoral conversion ... Excessive centralisation, rather than proving helpful, complicates the Church's life and her missionary outreach. (*EG*, 32)

In this context Francis proposed that episcopal conferences should have a juridical status so that they can have 'genuine doctrinal authority' (*EG*, 32). He made it clear that he wanted to undo the severe limitations that had been imposed on the effective authority of episcopal conferences by the 1998 *motu proprio 'Apostolos Suos'* of Pope John Paul II.

On 17 October 2015, Francis gave an important and radical address at a ceremony commemorating the fiftieth anniversary of the institution of the Synod of Bishops. In it he put forward the image of the Church as 'an inverted pyramid, [where] the top is located beneath the base'. He went on to say:

> The first level of the exercise of *synodality* is had in the particular Churches ... the presbyteral council, the college

of consultors, chapters of canons and the pastoral council. Only to the extent that these organisations keep connected to the 'base' and start from people and their daily problems, can a synodal Church begin to take shape.

He went on at once to emphasise the importance of developing what he called 'intermediary instances of *collegiality*' at the level of ecclesiastical provinces, regions, and conferences of bishops, 'perhaps by integrating and updating certain aspects of the ancient ecclesiastical organisation'. He said that the hope of the Vatican Council 'that such bodies would help to increase the spirit of episcopal *collegiality* has not yet been fully realised'. And he repeated the call he had already made in *Evangelii Gaudium* for 'a sound "decentralisation"'. He followed this by saying:

I am persuaded that in a synodal Church, greater light can be shed on the exercise of the Petrine primacy. The Pope is not, by himself, above the Church; but within it as one of the baptised, and within the College of Bishops as a Bishop among Bishops, called at the same time – as Successor of Peter – to lead the Church of Rome which presides in charity over all the Churches.

In these statements, and in a variety of widely quoted *obiter dicta* Francis overtly or tacitly acknowledged that some Vatican curia officials had overstepped the mark. He was clearly recognising that Catholic social teaching must apply not just to civil and political society but also to the Church itself. In this regard it is hard to avoid the conclusion that he was deliberately reaffirming the strong stance on issues of justice within the Church which had been taken at the 1971 Synod of Bishops – a synod whose teaching Vatican officials had ignored for forty years.

CHURCH UNITY

Ever since the Vatican Council the various popes have been committed to promoting ecumenism. However, Pope John Paul II and Pope Benedict XVI seemed to be reluctant to acknowledge the extent to which the highly centralised style of the present-day Catholic Church is an obstacle to Church unity. Many theologians and other committed Catholics had argued in vain for the Vatican to begin to implement the call of the council for collegiality. Francis has taken that call seriously.

But he has gone further. His use of the word 'synodality' alongside the word 'collegiality' is a major gesture of outreach and appreciation to the Orthodox Churches. He is saying that this is something that we Catholics – and especially the pope and the bishops – have to learn from these sister Churches. And, being Francis, he is not content with words. He is not even content with incorporating into his encyclical on the environment several beautiful passages from the statements of Patriarch Bartholomew. On 16 April 2016, he linked up with Bartholomew to visit asylum seekers in the Greek island of Lesbos, and his visit to the Patriarch in Istanbul was a particularly warm occasion of shared prayer and shared vision. He has also reached out warmly and generously to Orthodox leaders, such as Patriarch Kirill of Moscow and Catholicos Karekin II, the head of the Oriental Orthodox Armenian Apostolic Church, whose attitudes towards Rome had been one of greater reserve and some suspicion.

Francis has also developed a warm friendship with Archbishop Justin Welby, the symbolic head of the Anglican Communion. And on 31 October 2016 he travelled to Sweden to join Lutheran leaders in a joint commemoration of the five hundredth anniversary of the Protestant Reformation. However, the most original aspect of the commitment of Francis towards Church unity has been at the practical level. He has made a particular point of reaching out to Pentecostal and Evangelical Christians. He has engaged in public prayer sessions with them – and also with Catholic charismatics who have been looked at with some suspicion by many mainstream Catholic leaders on the grounds that they are unduly emotional and Pentecostal.

CLERICALISM

The firm commitment by Francis to the principles of subsidiarity and collegiality is closely linked to the frequently repeated condemnation by Francis of clericalism. Francis rehabilitated the Vatican II term 'people of God' which had fallen out of favour among Vatican officials in the previous twenty years; and he committed himself to trusting 'the people of God' and giving them an effective role in decision-making. He set out to work to bring about changes in Church structures and practices that would reflect this equality.

It is clear that for Francis the biggest obstacle to such empowerment of laypeople is *clericalism*. This includes an assumption that the priest is superior to 'ordinary' Christians, that he has a special status, that he deserves to be given various favours, that he knows what is best for 'his people', and that his decisions should not be questioned. It also involves belonging to a closed inner clerical circle who do not share their authority with others and who close ranks when they feel 'under attack' or are subjected to criticism. All of this is quite contrary to the ideal of priesthood which Francis repeatedly stressed.

For Pope Francis, the best way for a priest to avoid slipping into a clericalist mentality is to remain close to the people, especially to those who are poor and on the margins of society. As he said in a homily on 28 March 2013, during his first Holy Thursday as pope, the priest should have 'the smell of the sheep'.

In a letter of 12 January 2014 to the new cardinals, he issued a strong warning about the danger of clericalism. He went much further in an address to the members of the Vatican curia on 22 December 2014. In it he warned them against the danger of succumbing to what he called 'curial diseases'. He gave a quite detailed account of fifteen of these 'diseases'. The first of these is for officials to think they are indispensable, and immune to criticism. The second is excessive busyness. The third is what Francis called 'petrification' where they become mere 'paper-pushers'. Another is excessive planning and failure to leave space for the creative inspirations of the Holy Spirit. Yet another 'disease' is failure of the officials to work closely together. Then there is loss of one's first fervour, which Francis called 'spiritual Alzheimer's disease'.

Also included in his list were rivalry, hypocrisy, gossiping and grumbling, courting the favour of superiors, a selfish indifference to others and failure to share with and help those who are less experienced in the work. Near the end of his list he mentions glumness, lack of joy and courtesy, and excessive severity. Then come the accumulation of wealth and material goods, and the creation of exclusive cliques. The final 'disease' which Francis warns against is the accumulation of power and the use of this power to become rich or to gain yet more power. It is widely believed that by listing these possible diseases, Francis was in fact making a very severe criticism of the curia officials as he experienced them. Needless to say, his remarks gave rise to resentment among some of these officials.

It is important to point out that Francis is by no means content just to criticise the faults of curia officials. His major concern is to ensure that they live and act in a truly Christian manner. This concern is very evident in his decision on 9 November 2017 to establish a distinct section within the Vatican Secretariat of State. The title of this new subdivision is the 'Section for the Diplomatic Staff'. Its purpose is to provide 'more human, priestly, spiritual and professional accompaniment' to Vatican diplomats and those who are training to go into the Vatican diplomatic service.

CLERICAL SEX ABUSE

Probably the most controversial issue which has arisen in relation to the attitude and actions of Pope Francis is that of whether he has taken sufficiently seriously the issue of sexual abuse by priests. There cannot be any doubt that Francis himself is deeply upset about the damage that has been done to so many children and others.

It was particularly important that he would speak out strongly on the issue in Chile, where there has been huge anger about the abuse and about what many have seen as the failure by the bishops and by Francis himself to respond adequately. So, on the first day of his visit to Chile, 16 January 2018, he spoke in his address to the government authorities of his 'pain and shame … at the irreparable damage caused to children by some ministers of the Church' and of his commitment 'to ensuring that such things do not happen again'. That same day during his address to priests and members of religious communities, he spoke of 'the pain resulting from cases of abuse of minors' which he called 'this great and painful evil'. The director of the Vatican press office, Greg Burke, announced that on that afternoon Pope Francis met several people who had been abused by priests and that he prayed with them and also wept with them.

However, there was great anger in Chile and beyond when, a short time later, Francis again robustly defended his appointment of Bishop Barros who had been accused of witnessing the abuse by a priest of at least one young man and not reporting it. On this occasion he maintained that the accusation against Bishop Barros was a calumny. During the plane journey back from Peru to Rome, on 21 January 2018, Francis said he was sorry for the pain his choice of words had caused to victims of clerical abuse. He said that he should have pointed out that there is no *evidence* that the bishop is guilty, rather than saying that there is no *proof* of the bishop's guilt. This means that Francis was not insisting that all instances of abuse have to be *proved* conclusively, but that there is need for credible evidence to be put forward. He maintained that he had a duty to defend Bishop Barros because his case had been investigated and the investigators had not heard any credible evidence of his guilt.

There are a significant number of responsible commentators who maintain that the stance taken by Francis on this issue has been mistaken. They hold that during the years while he has been pope, he has responded quite inadequately on one crucial aspect of the clerical sex-abuse scandal. They say that he has been slow or unwilling to take effective action against bishops who turned a blind eye to the actions of abusing priests – bishops who moved these priests from one parish to another, or failed in various other ways to respond properly to the abuse. It has to be acknowledged that there is a significant difference between the present rapid and vigorous response of Church authorities to abusing priests and the apparent reluctance of the Vatican to discipline bishops who failed to respond adequately to clerical abuse in their dioceses. It seems that there is a hesitance in some parts of the Vatican curia to take effective action on this issue – and Francis has not yet succeeded in overcoming this resistance.

However, the Vatican press office issued a press release on 30 January 2018 saying that 'following recently received information' in regard to Bishop Barros, Pope Francis had arranged for Archbishop Scicluna 'to go to Santiago de Chile to hear those who have expressed their willingness to submit elements in their possession'. This news was widely welcomed – particularly because of the reputation of Archbishop Scicluna as deeply committed and objective in his dealings with issues of clerical sex abuse.

On 11 April 2018 the Vatican website published a letter that Pope Francis had written three days earlier to the bishops of Chile. In it he said that on 20 March Archbishop Scicluna, and Rev. Jordi Bertomeu Farnós, who had accompanied the Archbishop, had delivered to Francis their report, including their legal and pastoral assessment of the information which they had gathered. In his letter, Francis said that these two envoys told him that they themselves 'had been overwhelmed by the pain of so many victims of serious abuses'. Francis said that having carefully read their account he had to acknowledge that the testimonies collected by his envoys are witness to many 'crucified lives', which cause him to feel pain and shame. He said that he plans to call the bishops of Chile to Rome in order to discuss with them the conclusions of the report and his own conclusions, with the sole purpose of 'letting the truth shine out'. He then went on to say:

> For my own part, I acknowledge that I have made serious mistakes in the assessment and perception of the situation, especially due to a lack of truthful and balanced information. I now apologise to all those whom I have offended and I hope to be able to do it personally, in the coming weeks, in the meetings I will have with representatives of the people who were interviewed.

This letter indicates that Archbishop Scicluna has lived up to his reputation as a person who investigates clerical sex abuse with objectivity, courage and commitment. It also indicates that Pope Francis has fully accepted his report. I am not aware that any of the previous popes of the past century has, like Francis, publicly acknowledged that he has made serious mistakes on the clerical abuse issue and publicly issued a personal apology to those who have been hurt. It is not yet clear what disciplinary action Francis will take in relation to those who are named in the Scicluna report. But the obvious sincerity of his acceptance that he was mistaken and of his apology suggests that he will not hesitate to act on the report by taking decisive action in order to make amends and that he will do his best to bring healing to the troubled Church in Chile.

There can be no doubt that there is a link between clericalism and clerical sex abuse. Abusing priests use the power they have been given as clerics to take advantage of vulnerable people. If Pope Francis succeeds in his 'campaign' against clericalism, this should help to lessen this danger. However, it must be added that clericalism is not just a *moral* problem; it is also a *structural* problem. The institutional Church has a clericalist structure, in which the clergy have a power which is not given to laypeople. This provides a foundation for the abuse of this power by priests. So long as this clericalist structure remains, there is a danger that some priests will be guilty of clericalism, leading to the possibility or likelihood of clerical sex abuse.

Chapter Nine

The Nature and Role of Women

Pope Francis has never made any secret of the fact that women have played a key role in his life. During most of his childhood he lived in close proximity to his grandmother; and she had a major and lasting influence on him. During a general audience on 11 March 2015 he said: 'I still treasure the words my grandmother wrote to me on the day of my ordination. I carry them with me to this day inside my breviary.' Francis has also spoken of the fact that as a teenager he fell in love with a young woman and considered marrying her. Like many Catholics in Latin America he has a very deep devotion to the Blessed Virgin Mary, and on his overseas travels he never fails to visit the local Marian shrine.

Francis is very much in line with recent Catholic social teaching in speaking out strongly against the injustices which are suffered by women. And, being Francis, he is not content to speak in generalities on the issue; he likes to give concrete examples. One striking instance came in his address to thousands of people in a poverty-stricken and flood-devastated area on the outskirts of Trujillo, Peru on 20 January 2018. Knowing that in Latin America there are many instances of femicide (killing of women) he said:

I want to invite you to combat a scourge that affects our American continent: the numerous cases where women are killed. And the many situations of violence that are kept quiet behind so many walls. I ask you to fight against this source of suffering by calling for legislation and a culture that repudiates every form of violence.

However, some of the occasional spontaneous remarks by Francis about women have at times evoked criticism from feminists. Even those of us who admire him greatly are inclined to cringe when we hear these remarks. We who live in the English-speaking world are particularly sensitive to any statement which shows that the speaker displays a residual trace of a patriarchal or sexist attitude. We must recognise that in many other cultures the development of this kind of awareness is much less advanced. Pope Francis comes from a Latin-American culture which has traditionally been quite patriarchal and even 'macho'. So we should not be too surprised if some of his remarks about women come across as insensitive or archaic. Against this background those who admire him can perhaps forgive him for making a tactless remark to members of the European parliament in Strasbourg on 25 November 2014. Describing the situation in Europe he said: 'In many quarters we encounter a general impression of weariness and aging, of a Europe which is now a "grandmother", no longer fertile and vibrant.'

In his first major document, *Evangelii Gaudium*, Pope Francis said: 'The Church acknowledges the indispensable contribution which women make to society through the sensitivity, intuition and other distinctive skill sets which they, more than men, tend to possess' (103). He went on to acknowledge that many women offer 'new contributions to theological reflection'. However, in the following paragraph he said: 'Demands that the legitimate rights of women be respected, based on the firm conviction that men and women are equal in dignity, present the Church with profound and challenging questions which cannot be lightly evaded' (*EG*, 104). Then he added: 'The reservation of the priesthood to males, as a sign of Christ the Spouse who gives himself in the Eucharist, is not a question open to discussion, but it can prove especially divisive if sacramental power is too closely identified with power in general.' He noted that sacramental power is not a power of domination and does not make a priest superior to other Christians.

The following year, in an address to the members of the International Theological Commission on 5 December 2014, Francis noted that there were now a small number of women among this group and he said that there is a need for more to join them. He said that 'by virtue of their feminine genius, women theologians can detect, to the benefit of all, certain unexplored aspects of the unfathomable mystery of Christ ... I invite you to derive the greatest benefit of this specific contribution of women to the understanding of the faith.'

In using the phrase 'feminine genius' Francis presumably had in mind 'the sensitivity, intuition and other distinctive skill sets' which he mentioned in *Evangelii Gaudium*. This phrase, borrowed from Pope John Paul II's 'Letter on Women' on 29 June 1995, is quite controversial. Some women see its use by Church leaders as a way of justifying the view that by nature women are different from men and that only men are by nature suitable to be priests. Another argument that has been put forward by Catholic authorities to explain why women cannot be ordained is that the priest acts 'in the person of Christ' and that only a male priest can do that. When the validity of these two arguments are called in question, Church authorities respond by pointing out that Jesus chose only men to be priests and that the tradition of the Church has never allowed women to become priests.

There are indications that Pope Francis accepted the validity of at least the second and third of these arguments. During the return journey to Rome from Sweden on 1 November 2016, he was asked whether there was a realistic possibility that there would be women priests in the Catholic Church in the next few decades; and if not, why not. In his brief response he simply said, 'The last clear word was given by Saint John Paul II, and this holds.' It is clear that for him this is a closed issue.

HIS VIEW ABOUT FEMININE QUALITIES

On 7 February 2015 Francis gave an address to participants in the plenary assembly of the Pontifical Council for Culture. In it he gave an interesting and fairly comprehensive account of his concept of the nature of women and the relationship between women and men. He maintained that we have now moved on from a model 'of pure and simple *parity*, applied mechanically, and of absolute *equality*'. Now 'a new paradigm has emerged, that of *reciprocity*, in equivalence and difference'. Women and men 'possess an identical nature, but each with its own modality'. Each of them 'is necessary for the other, and vice versa, for they truly complete the fullness of the person'.

He went on to say:

I note and I encourage the contribution of so many women who work within the family, in the areas of teaching the faith, pastoral work, schooling, but also in social, cultural and economic structures. You women know how to embody the tender face of God, his mercy … to welcome rather than to exclude. In this sense, I like to describe the feminine dimension of the Church as the welcoming womb which regenerates life.

Francis set out to provide a balanced picture of what he sees as the role of women. On the one hand, he stressed 'the irreplaceable role of the woman *in the family*' and maintained that women have 'qualities of delicacy, particular sensitivity and tenderness' which are 'a genuine strength for the life of the family,' producing 'a climate of serenity and harmony'.

On the other hand, he stressed the importance 'of encouraging and fostering the effective presence of women in many areas of the *public sphere*, in the world of work and in places where important decisions are made'. But this is to be done 'while at the same time maintaining their presence and preferential and wholly special attention in and for the family'. He said that 'all institutions, including the ecclesial community, are called to guarantee the freedom of choice of women, so they may have the opportunity to assume social and ecclesial responsibilities, in a manner in harmony with family life'.

In selecting short passages from this address I have deliberately quoted the words of Francis himself in order to convey his thoughts as accurately as possible. It is clear that he fully accepts a concept of the nature and role of women which is quite closely in line with the teaching of Pope John Paul II on what he called 'the genius of women'. It is one that holds that, although both women and men are equally human, women have a set of qualities, such as tenderness and sensitivity, which give a particular 'modality' to their way of being human.

This understanding of 'the nature of women' is rejected by many feminists and others – not merely theologians but also psychologists, sociologists and anthropologists. There are, of course, many who accept that it is generally the case that women tend to be rather more sensitive than men in relating to others. But they may not be sure to what extent this is a matter of biology rather than of cultural conditioning. What is widely rejected is the kind of *conclusions* that are frequently drawn by Church leaders from this notion of a distinctive 'genius of women'. They object particularly to the conclusion that the distinctive qualities of women mean that it is only men who can act *in persona Christi* and can therefore be ordained as priests.

Chapter Ten

A Challenging Dialogue with Women

Even though Francis says that the issue of priestly ordination of women is 'a closed issue', this leaves open two other questions:

- » How can women be given more responsible roles in the running of the Church?
- » Can women be ordained as deacons?

These two topics were openly discussed when Francis engaged in dialogue with a leadership group of religious sisters. The UISG is an organisation which brings together the top leadership of religious congregations of women from all over the world. Francis met with them on 12 May 2016. They had bravely asked that instead of listening to a speech from him they would have this opportunity to have a dialogue with him. And he agreed to this proposal to face questions from this group of highly articulate women who had strong views about the position of women in the Church and had plenty of experience of exercising authority in their own congregations.

Having asked for input from their sisters all over the world, the UISG leaders formulated a number of key questions to put to the Pope. The very first question was worded diplomatically, but was in fact a serious challenge to him on the issue of how women could exercise leadership in the Church. Their spokesperson said:

Pope Francis, you said that 'the feminine genius is needed in all expressions in the life of society ... and in the Church', and yet women are excluded from decision-making processes in the Church, especially at the highest levels, and from preaching at the Eucharist. An important obstacle to the Church's full embrace of 'feminine genius' is the bond that decision-making processes and preaching both have with priestly ordination. Do you see a way of separating leadership roles and preaching at the Eucharist from ordination, so that our Church can be more open to receiving the genius of women in the very near future?

Francis responded very honestly. He shared his conviction that women can and should be given leadership roles in the Church. He said: 'It is true that women are excluded from decision-making processes in the Church: not excluded, but the presence of women is very weak there, in decision-making processes.' So he added, 'We must move forward.' He went on to note that a religious sister manages the secretariat of the Pontifical Council for Justice and Peace, and suggested that other similar opportunities could and would arise for women. He said that 'for many aspects of decision-making processes ordination is not necessary'.

However, Francis was equally honest, though not always very clear, in sharing what he saw as the difficulty. As he explained it, the difficulty arises from the fact that some leadership or authority roles are linked to ordination and cannot be exercised by women since women cannot be ordained. So he said that there is no problem about having a woman preach at a Liturgy of the Word. But they are not allowed to preach at the Eucharistic Celebration because in the Eucharist there is a unity between the Liturgy of the Word and the Eucharistic Liturgy – and only an ordained priest can preside at this celebration. Francis added: 'The priest or bishop who presides does so in the person of Jesus Christ.' Obviously aware that this is a highly controversial point, Francis added, 'But it is possible to study and explain further what I have just said very quickly and rather simply.' A little later he came back to this point saying, 'I do not have sufficient theology or clarity to explain it now.' He acknowledged that it is a mystery, and he added immediately: 'It is the mystery of Christ's presence, and the priest or the bishop celebrates *in persona Christi.*'

Francis moved on to more comfortable ground when he went on emphasise the important role that women play in the discussion and reflection process leading up to the authoritative decision. He said: 'The way of viewing a problem, of seeing anything, is different for a woman compared to a man. They must be complementary, and in consultations it is important that there are women.' He illustrated this by citing his own experience of decision-making when he was archbishop in Buenos Aires.

Returning to the issue of giving women more leadership roles in the Church, Francis said, 'We must go forward in that area, prudently, but seeking solutions.' He then went on to refer to two dangers which must be avoided. The first of these, he said, is feminism: 'We must not fall into feminism, because this would reduce a woman's importance.' He said that the role of a woman in the Church is based, not on feminism, but on her 'right as a baptised person, with the charisms and the gifts that the Spirit has given'. In a subsequent interview Sr Carmen Sammut, the president of the UISG, interpreted this rather obscure remark. She suggested that Francis was saying that women should not want to be leaders simply because they are women.

Francis moved on quickly to what he saw as the second danger. This is clericalism. He was highly critical of the fact that many parish priests fail to obey the law of the Church which clearly lays down that they must have 'a council of laypeople, for and with lay men, women and women religious for pastoral ministry and financial affairs'. He added:

> Clericalism is a negative attitude. And it requires complicity: it is something done by two parties, just as it takes two to dance the tango … That is: the priest wants to clericalise the layman, the laywoman, the man or woman religious, and the layperson asks to be clericalised, because it is easier that way.

Interestingly, Francis insisted that in a parish it would be wrong to ordain an excellent man who is a good organiser as a deacon. He should remain a layman because he could be 'clericalised' if he were made a deacon.

THE DIACONATE ISSUE

In their next question to Francis the women took up this issue of the diaconate: 'What prevents the Church from including women among permanent deacons, as was the case in the primitive Church? Why not constitute an official commission to study the matter?' In his reply Francis acknowledged that there were some deaconesses in the early Church. 'But', he asked, 'what were these deaconesses? Were they ordained or not?' He went on to say: 'I would like to constitute an official commission to study the question: I think it will be good for the Church to clarify this point.' A little later he added: 'So then, with regard to the diaconate, yes, I think that it is useful to have a commission that clarifies this area properly, especially with regard to the early times of the Church.' Not long after the meeting Pope Francis did set up a very balanced commission to study this issue.

In their third question the sisters' spokesperson asked: 'What role could the International Union of Superiors General (UISG) play, in order to have a say in the thinking of the Church, a word that is listened to, given that it conveys the voices of two thousand institutes of women religious?' And she went on to ask bluntly: 'Can the Church afford to continue speaking about us, instead of speaking with us?'

Before responding to this specific question Francis roundly condemned parish priests who use religious sisters just to look after the priest's house rather than being involved in some genuine apostolate of service such as catechetical work. For the priest to treat the sisters in this way, said Francis, is servitude rather than service. It demeans the life and dignity of those women.

By way of responding to the question of what role UISG can play in the Church, Francis said that a consecrated woman is an icon of the Church, an icon of Mary; whereas a priest is not an icon of the Church or of Mary. He then insisted strongly that 'the Church is feminine; the Church is woman'. So he maintained that the distinctive role which religious sisters play in the Church is that by their consecration into the religious life they become an icon of the Church and an icon of Our Lady – a role which men cannot do. Francis added rather lamely, 'I hope this does not elude you' – perhaps because he sensed that some of the sisters were not convinced that he had provided an adequate answer to the question about how the voices of so many sisters from all over the world could be heard more effectively in the Vatican.

Francis then went on to respond to the challenging question of whether the Church can afford to continue speaking *about* the sisters, instead of speaking *with* them. He said he agreed completely with the point of the question:

> The hierarchy ... of the Church must speak about you, but firstly and presently ... must speak with you. This is certain ... Yes, yes! I will communicate this to the Prefect: you must be present in the Assembly! It is clear, because to speak about someone who is absent is not even evangelical: one must be able to hear, to listen to what is being thought, and then act together. I agree. I did not imagine such separation, honestly. Thank you for having said it so courageously and with that smile. ... We need to hear the sisters because they have another way of looking at things. That is what I was saying before: it is important that you always be included ... Thank you for the question.

The sisters' spokesperson then asked the fourth question. She noted that sisters find themselves obstructed by canon law in their efforts to renew their way of life and structures. Francis responded by assuring them that changes could easily be made in the Church's laws – but he went on to speak at considerable length about the great importance of prayerful personal and shared discernment, prior to making any changes.

Another part of this question related to the difficulty young people today have in making a permanent commitment. The sisters asked: 'Can we be open somehow to temporary commitments?' In the course of his lengthy reply Francis said: 'I would be in favour of prolonging temporary vows a little, because of this culture of the provisional that young people experience these days.'

There were other written questions which were not read out. They had to do mainly with money issues. Francis spoke at some length both about how wrong it was for people to have to pay in order to be allowed to receive the sacraments and about how important it is for those who have taken religious vows to avoid luxury and practise genuine poverty. The sisters said: 'Women religious do not receive a stipend for their services, as priests do ... How can we find the financial resources necessary to fulfil our mission?' The key part of the extended reply of Francis was:

> Where there are conflicts over what the local Churches ask of you, you need to pray, to discern and to have the courage, when necessary, to say 'no'; and to have the generosity, when necessary, to say 'yes'. But you see how discernment is necessary in every case!

Francis went on to hear of a further difficulty which the sisters put before him. They told him that some Church authorities do not approve of their commitment to their prophetic ministry of being in solidarity with the poor and the marginalised. They consider that in doing so the sisters are just being social activists, or are assuming political stances. So they hold that the sisters should concentrate more on a kind of mystical life.

In response Francis said that of course all religious sisters 'should live mystically'. But he assured them that being a mystic is not the same as being a mummy! He encouraged those whose charism is to work with the poor or with refugees to act in accordance with that charism – even if people call them communists when they engage in that ministry. He went on to tell them how, when he was archbishop in Argentina, a religious sister was accused by the military dictatorship of being a communist because of her work in rescuing girls. She had even been slandered in a report to Rome and had received a reproof from Rome. Francis told how he offered her effective support, by telling her that she should continue her work in obedience to him as the local authority, rather than obeying 'a letter that comes from twelve thousand kilometres away'.

No doubt some of the sisters would have felt that this response of Francis did not really resolve the problem which arises when *local* religious authorities disapprove of the sisters' prophetic ministry. But at least it showed them that Francis' heart was with them and gave them some encouragement in facing the difficulty.

In his concluding remarks Francis encouraged them to rest and said kind words about the wisdom and prayer life of their older sisters. He then added: 'I like hearing questions, because they make me think and I feel like a goalkeeper who stands there, waiting for the ball from wherever it comes ... The things

I have promised to do I will do.' Some of the sisters may have felt that his image of being a goalkeeper suggested an unduly defensive attitude, but clearly that was not his intention.

The most important elements which emerged from this lengthy interchange with the religious sisters were that Francis welcomed the opportunity to engage in genuine dialogue with women, particularly with religious sisters, that he sympathised with their difficulties, that he was willing to be challenged, and that he learned from their challenges on key issues and undertook to remedy problems.

Francis did not promise to make the more radical changes that some of the sisters and other Catholic women might have wished for. For instance, they might have noted that, despite his assurances that Church laws can be changed, he did not undertake to change canon 124. This is the law which effectively states that only those who are in sacred orders are capable of exercising the power of governance or jurisdiction in the Church.

It is quite likely that at least some of the sisters were rather disappointed at some of his answers and comments – perhaps especially at the very negative interpretation he gave of the word 'feminism'. Some of the sisters may also have seen more clearly that male religious leaders – even those as open-minded and saintly as Pope Francis – still have blind spots in their understanding of the feelings and concerns of women. And this might have increased their conviction that the Catholic Church needs, now more than ever, to allow women to play a full role in all aspects of Church life.

However, the willingness of Francis to engage in serious dialogue and to allow himself to be challenged would have given encouragement to religious sisters and to other non-ordained committed women and men to continue their efforts to ensure that their voices are heard more effectively in the Catholic Church.

A HOPE FOR THE FUTURE

Over the past twenty years I have spent many hours working with women in various groups. Listening to their concerns, and to those of women friends and relatives, has led me to add the following further reflections on what committed Christian women might hope for from Pope Francis.

Francis is obviously very deeply concerned about particular categories of women – for instance, those who are trafficked for sexual exploitation. His address to the diplomatic corps on 8 January 2018 shows that he has real concern for women 'who repeatedly suffer from violence and oppression, even within their own families'. Furthermore, I have no doubt that his own experience has convinced him that women suffer even more seriously than men as a result of poverty. But it is not clear that the second-class position of *all* women in society – and particularly in the Church – has become a top priority for him.

The other chapters in this book show, I hope, that Francis has taken a radical stance on two of the most crucial issues in our world today: he has taken an uncompromising 'option for the poor' and 'option for the earth'. My sense is that many women feel sad and disappointed that, up to the present at least, there is no evidence that he has taken an equally radical 'option for women'. I have to reluctantly admit that, despite my admiration for Francis on so many issues, I share their view on this crucial issue.

Francis believes that in order to respond adequately to the problem of poverty and to take a stance on caring for the earth, we need to undergo a real *conversion*. Although he is more open than his predecessors to listening to the views of women and to giving them some more important roles in the Vatican curia, I cannot honestly say that his words and actions show that his option for women is as far-reaching as his option for the earth and for the poor. A truly radical conversion has three major components. It includes a change at the intellectual level; that, is, a change in our *thinking*, a 'turning around' and 'seeing the world with new eyes' (Macy and Brown, 135–6). This leads on to a change in our *moral behaviour*, the way we *act*. And these two changes are largely underpinned by an *affective* change – the way we *feel* about the issue.

Suppose Francis were to make a radical option on behalf of women. An immediate practical consequence could be that he would, on his own initiative (*motu proprio*), change the Church law, canon 124, which precludes women from exercising juridical power in the Church. He could then appoint several women to very senior management positions in the Vatican itself. After all, nobody could seriously deny that there are plenty of women, including laywomen and members of religious communities, who have all the skills and experience required to exercise such roles effectively. We could then expect that some of these senior management women would be named as cardinals. Of course it would be much better if senior Church leaders adopted a modified version of the democratic and participatory leadership system widely used by congregations of vowed religious.[1] But so long as the hierarchical model continues to be used, it is necessary that women take senior positions within it.

The immediate effect would be that the challenging dialogue which Francis had with the leaders of congregations of religious women would no longer be highly unusual. The unanswered or unasked questions of that dialogue would be dealt with on a daily basis. At the highest Church level, dialogue and joint decision-making, in which married and unmarried lay women and members of religious communities would be included, would be an everyday occurrence. The practice of regular discussions and planning meetings in which women would have an equal voice could go a long way to ensuring that Francis himself and other male Church leaders would have fewer blind spots in relation to the feelings and concerns of women. Even before the issue of the ordination of women was resolved, it would become evident that the phrase 'Church leaders' would no longer apply exclusively to male celibates.

Another example: Francis could immediately publish the report of the commission on the diaconate. If the report declares that there were *ordained* women deacons in the early Church, he could at once call for the ordination of suitably qualified women as deacons. We would then be spared the painful experience of seeing Church leaders in the Western world attempting to solve or alleviate the problem of the shortage of priests by choosing married men (only men) to play significant roles as deacons in

---

1 Every six years, the members elect delegates who meet together for a few weeks to decide on the congregation's policy and directions for the next six years; they then elect a leadership *team* to implement these policies; the leaders 'return to the ranks' when their term in office has expired.

Church ceremonies, while leaving even the most gifted women still silent down in the Church benches. Furthermore, Francis could then establish a commission whose task would be to issue a report fairly soon on whether the acceptance of ordained deacons had effectively re-opened the issue of the ordination of women to the priesthood.

WHAT A GIFT IT WOULD BE

If this were to happen it would be a wonderful gift first of all to our Church. It would be a major step in the dismantling of the clericalism which Francis believes to be so damaging to the preaching of the Gospel. Secondly, these changes in the Church would have a major influence in the wider world. It would mean that the challenge of Church leaders to the many injustices to which women are subjected would no longer ring hollow as they do at present. Pope Francis would have great credibility in calling for a quite radical conversion in relation to the way women are seen and treated in society.

Of course, there would be those in the Church who would be quite scandalised by such changes and who would oppose it in every way they could. But it is likely that this opposition would come mainly from the relatively small number of those who are already resisting Francis – and not succeeding in causing him to abandon his agenda. And even if there were some increase in the number of his opponents, it is very likely that this would be more than compensated for by a huge tide of support for such new initiatives from millions of Catholics who feel ashamed that, in the Church as it is at present, women are left in a second-class position. Furthermore, as Christians we must say that, ultimately, changes should not be decided on the basis of calculations of this kind. As a leader of deep personal conviction and great courage, Francis would surely follow the principle *Fiat justitia ruat cælum*, which means that justice must be done 'even if the heavens should fall' – in other words, regardless of consequences.

Many of us who are enthused by the radical commitment of Pope Francis to hearing 'the cry of the earth and the cry of the poor' might be tempted to say that we should be willing to wait before we call for him to hear, in an equally radical way, the cry of women for justice in the Church and in society. But this is not a defensible position. The fact is that there is a fundamental link between an option for women, an option for the poor, and an option for the earth.

There is one key insight that has emerged from feminist theology in recent times. It concerns the all-pervading effect of the *patriarchy* which has marred society for centuries, and which is still a major feature of most cultures in our world. We have come to recognise that patriarchy does not merely underpin the injustices suffered by women but that it is also a major factor in the *other* structural injustices of our society. Patriarchal attitudes are a driving force in the despoiling of the earth and in the marginalisation of so many people in every continent of our world. I am not suggesting that women are by nature less inclined to act unjustly. But the reality is that the present unjust and exploitative structures of our world have been created almost entirely by men; and this system has been shaped by patriarchal attitudes.

Furthermore, we need to recognise that clericalism is a particularly damaging version of patriarchy. Pope Francis has condemned it strongly and repeatedly. But the basis of clericalism in the structures of the institutional Church remains firmly in place. When a pope dies or resigns, male cardinals meet to elect a new pope; the advisory group set up by Francis is all men, synods of bishops in Rome are made up almost entirely of men, and national episcopal conferences decide on policies and laws for the local Churches. Moreover, canon law insists that even pastoral councils in parishes are only advisory; this is because canon 124 of the Church legal system precludes women from exercising juridical power in the Church.

The present clerical structures make it impossible for women to take their rightful place in decision-making at every level in the Church. It means too that the distinctive biological and cultural experiences and concerns of women, especially in sexual matters, are not adequately taken account of in official Catholic teaching on key moral issues. But it also gives rise to far more serious issues which are seldom publicly acknowledged. In practically every part of the world, some priests use their privileged clerical status to abuse women sexually.

Francis had a dialogue with his Jesuit confreres in Peru on 19 January 2018. In the course of it he said that the Catholic Church must hear from those who have been abused by clergy. 'We need to listen to what someone who has been abused feels.' He went on to reveal that he himself usually meets a group of such abused women on Fridays. He added that women in this situation have a very difficult time: 'They are annihilated.' If many other senior Church-men were to follow this example of Francis by listening to the stories of a group of women who had been abused by clergy, it might wake them up to the baleful consequences of the clericalist patriarchal structures of our Church and could, hopefully, lead to a dismantlement of these structures.

The interlocking structures of oppression in our world must be recognised by Christians, especially Church leaders, by hearing the cry of the earth, the cry of the poor, and the cry of women. And our Christian faith calls us to respond to this triple cry of pain by opening our hearts and minds to God's transforming gift of metanoia, a conversion of heart and mind, of behaviour and structures. This one single conversion has three distinct 'faces'. The option for the poor and the option for the earth will always remain incomplete until they are accompanied by a quite radical option for women. So our hope for Pope Francis is not that he will undergo some new or different conversion but that he will fill out this somewhat less developed aspect of his present conversion which is so radical and authentic in relation to the poor and the earth. As we pray for him we can dare to invite him to draw out the full implications of an invitation he himself issued in *Laudato Si'*.

In that encyclical he asks us 'to become painfully aware, to dare to turn what is happening to the world into our own personal suffering' (*LS*, 19). One key aspect of 'what is happening to our world' is that women are suffering from injustice not only in secular society but also in the Church. If Francis and other Church leaders (and we men wherever we are) are willing to allow ourselves to feel the pain of women, then this will enable us to have some sense of what our sisters feel. This in turn will provide a foundation for us to 'see the world with new eyes' – to see reality as women see it. Only then can we have a realistic hope that things will change for women into a situation where,

'Mercy and truth have met; justice and peace have kissed; truth will spring up from the earth, and justice look down from heaven' (Ps 85:10–11).

Chapter Eleven

The Liturgy Issue

There is one quite striking example of the determination of Francis to ensure that the members of the Vatican curia must respect the practise of subsidiarity and collegiality. It involved the relationship between him and Cardinal Sarah, the head of the Vatican department which deals with liturgy.

The Vatican Council authorised the use of local languages in the liturgy. Guidelines for such translations were spelled out in 1969 by the 'Consilium for Implementing the Constitution on Sacred Liturgy' in a document called *Comme Le Prévoit*. This laid down that a true translation does not have to follow the Latin text word for word; it must communicate to a particular people the original meaning of the text, using their own idiom. Just a few years later, a translation of the text of the Mass into English was prepared in some haste by the International Commission for English in the Liturgy (ICEL). The translators carefully followed the guidelines of *Comme Le Prévoit*. This text was used in the Catholic Church for the next forty years.

However, before too long it was recognised that this English translation was not perfect. The ICEL liturgical and theological experts spent many years working on preparing a new translation. In 1998, this revised translation was approved by the various conferences of bishops in English-speaking countries. However, when it was sent to Rome for final approval, it was rejected by the Vatican's Congregation for Divine Worship and the Discipline of the Sacraments.

This rejection came about as a result of two major changes which had occurred under the papacy of Pope John Paul II. The first of these was an ever-increasing centralisation of power in the Vatican curia. The authority of national conferences of bishops, and of individual bishops, was gradually undermined. This meant that the Vatican Council's emphasis on the collegiality of the worldwide bishops was effectively ignored. The second major change was a movement or approach which came to be called 'The Reform of the Reform'. This was a concerted effort by many powerful Vatican figures, and some conservative Church figures in different parts of the world, to roll back some of the liturgical changes called for by Vatican II. One of the main aims of this group was to reject the guidelines on translation laid down in the 1969 document *Comme Le Prévoit.*

The Reform of the Reform had a major success when the Congregation for Divine Worship and the Discipline of the Sacraments issued the document *Liturgiam Authenticam* ('Authentic Liturgy') in 2001. This new document insisted that liturgical translations must follow the Latin very closely. It called into question the long years of work of ICEL. In July of that year Rome established a group called *Vox Clara* ('Clear Voice') to supervise the translation of liturgical texts into the English language (John Wilkins in O'Collins 2017, 14). This group effectively undermined the competence of ICEL. Furthermore, the membership of ICEL was partly changed, to give it a more conservative complexion.

The new ICEL group followed the prescriptions of the 2001 Vatican document *Liturgiam Authenticam* and in 2009, the eleven English-speaking conferences of bishops submitted to Rome an extremely literal translation. The Vatican liturgy department authorities then made further thousands of changes in this translation. 'No dialogue or discussion took place before the radically changed text was returned as the final approved text' (Bergin 2017, 605). This highly Latinised and difficult translation was then imposed on the Catholic Churches of the English-speaking world.

CARDINAL SARAH AND POPE FRANCIS

Cardinal Sarah is the current head of the Vatican department which had issued the *Liturgiam Authenticam* document. He had been transferred by Pope Francis from his former role as the head of a Vatican agency called *Cor Unum* which, during the papacy of Pope Benedict XVI, had attempted (and partly succeeded) in limiting the freedom of action of *Caritas Internationalis*. Cardinal Sarah adopted a very conservative stance in relation to the liturgy. For instance, he maintained that priests should celebrate Mass facing eastward, with their back to the people. Pope Francis went to the trouble of correcting him on this point.

There was widespread dissatisfaction among Catholics with the Vatican insistence on imposing unduly literal translations on bishops' conferences. It is clear that Francis agreed with those who held that this excessive exercise of curial authority over national and local conferences of bishops amounted to a rejection of the commitment to collegiality by the Vatican Council. So, on 3 September 2017, Francis issued an apostolic letter entitled *Magnum Principium*.

In its very first paragraph this document stated that the council has 'entrusted to the bishops … the weighty task of introducing the vernacular language into the liturgy and of preparing and approving the versions of the liturgical books'. It went on to restore this task to the episcopal conferences in various parts of the world. It did so by making a fundamental change in canon 838 of the Church's Code of Canon Law. A key passage comes in the revised version of this canon:

> It pertains to the Episcopal Conferences to *faithfully* prepare versions of the liturgical books in vernacular languages, suitably *accommodated* within defined limits, and *to approve* and *publish the liturgical books for the regions for which they are responsible after the confirmation of the Apostolic See.*

The effect of this is that the role of Cardinal Sarah's department is simply to review and confirm translations authorised by the bishops, in a spirit of trust and collaboration. The Vatican curia was no longer entitled to impose translations on bishops' conferences all over the world.

Quite extraordinarily, Cardinal Sarah published an article just a month later in which he maintained that the Pope's new document did not replace the Vatican's *Liturgiam Authenticam* document of 2001. He claimed that the *confirmatio* from Rome is actually almost synonymous with a *recognitio*, which in effect would mean that his department would still be entitled to correct and change any translations authorised by the bishops.

On 17 October 2017 Francis took the very unusual step of issuing a public correction to Cardinal Sarah. He wrote and published a letter to the cardinal pointing out that certain articles in the 2001 document were clearly abrogated by the Pope's new *Magnum Principium* document. He also said: 'One cannot say that *recognitio* and *confirmatio* are "strictly synonymous" or "interchangeable."' He went on to say:

> *Magnum Principium* no longer holds that the translations must be in conformity on all points with the norms of *Liturgiam authenticam*, as was done in the past … Thus it is clear that certain numbers of LA were repealed or were rendered out-dated and reformulated by the new canon.

In this letter, Francis also insisted on what is meant by a 'faithful' translation. He said this word *fideliter* 'implies a threefold fidelity: [1] to the original text *in primis* (= above all); [2] to the particular language into which it is translated; and finally [3] to the intelligibility of the text for the recipients.'

This clarification by the Pope of what is required of a 'faithful' translation is extremely important. It gives a mandate to those who are translating the texts in different regions of the world to take account both of the peculiarities of language usage in different cultures and of the limits to the comprehension of people who could not be expected to be familiar with obscure Latinised words like 'consubstantial'. Here Francis was reaffirming the fact that the translators are now set free from the slavish word-for-word verbal echoing in English and other languages of the Latin words of the text which had been insisted on by Cardinal Sarah's department.

This strong action by Francis is particularly significant for two distinct reasons. Firstly, it shows his sensitivity to the real needs of so-called 'ordinary' people – especially of poor people; in this case their need for a liturgical language that they can readily understand and that touches their hearts. Secondly, it clearly shows how determined he is to undo the excessive centralisation of power in the Vatican and to bring about an 'on the ground' implementation of the Vatican II commitment to the collegiality of bishops.

Section Two

AN ECOLOGICAL SPIRITUALITY

Chapter Twelve

A New Emphasis on Ecology

From the very beginning of his papacy Francis showed a particular concern for the environment. On 16 March 2013, just three days after he had been elected, he told journalists that he had chosen the name of Francis of Assisi, because 'Francis was a man of poverty, who loved and protected creation'. Three days later, he linked protection of people with protection of the environment, pointing out that being a protector 'means protecting all creation, the beauty of the created world'; and he added: 'Everything has been entrusted to our protection, and all of us are responsible for it.' His linking of concern for the exploited earth with concern for victims and for marginalised and exploited people has been a consistent theme. It is clear, then, that Francis is inviting us to act in solidarity not merely with excluded and fragile humans, but also with non-human creatures and the whole of the fragile ecosystem. This expanded range of meaning of the word 'solidarity' is a key to understanding his teaching on the environment.

On 5 June 2013, UN World Environment Day, Francis devoted his General Audience message to the topic of care for the earth. Condemning 'consumerism' and a 'culture of waste', he called for 'a spirit of solidarity grounded in our common responsibility for the earth and for all our brothers and sisters in the human family'. He spoke of the importance of holding on to an attitude of wonder, contemplation, and listening to creation. Then, as on previous occasions, he called for people 'to respect and care for creation, to be attentive to every person, to oppose the culture of wastefulness and waste, and to promote a culture of solidarity and encounter'.

In his *Urbi et Orbi* message on Easter Sunday 2013, Francis said, 'Let us be ... channels through which God can water the earth, protect all creation and make justice and peace flourish.' Fifteen months later, on 21 September 2014, during his address to civil authorities in Tirana, Albania, he again linked human solidarity with respect for creation: 'Alongside the globalisation of the markets there must also be a corresponding globalisation of solidarity; together with economic growth there must be a greater respect for creation.'

On 28 July 2013, Francis gave an address to the bishops of Brazil. He recalled the gathering of the Latin American and Caribbean bishops in Aparecida which drew up the CELAM 2007 document. Francis himself had been a major architect of that document. It had underscored the dangers facing the Amazon environment and the indigenous people living there. In this context Francis called for 'respect and protection of the entire creation which God has entrusted to humanity'. He went on to say that creation should not be 'indiscriminately exploited but rather made into a garden'. His address gave encouragement to indigenous people from the Amazon region, whom he met and who have been resisting the encroachment on the forest by ranchers, farmers, and agribusiness enterprises.

It might seem surprising that Francis devoted only a small section of *Evangelii Gaudium* to the topic of ecology. This was perhaps partly because that document was a response to what had emerged in the 2012 Synod of Bishops on the new evangelisation, where the environment had not been a major issue. It may also be that the Pope was holding back on this topic because of his intention to treat it much more comprehensively in an encyclical.

In *Evangelii Gaudium*, the Pope's first reference to the topic of ecology comes when he says, 'Whatever is fragile, like the environment, is defenceless before the interests of a deified market' (*EG*, 56). Later in the document he says:

> There are other weak and defenceless beings who are frequently at the mercy of economic interests or indiscriminate exploitation. I am speaking of creation as a whole. We human beings are not only the beneficiaries but also the stewards of other creatures. Thanks to our bodies, God has joined us so closely to the world around us that we can feel the desertification of the soil almost as a physical ailment, and the extinction of a species as a painful disfigurement. Let us not leave in our wake a swathe of destruction and death which will affect our own lives and those of future generations. (*EG*, 215)

He then says: 'Small yet strong in the love of God, like St Francis of Assisi, all of us, as Christians, are called to watch over and protect the fragile world in which we live, and all its peoples' (*EG*, 216).

Francis took up the topic, again rather briefly, in his Peace Message for 2014. He referred to 'the devastation of natural resources and ongoing pollution'. He then went on to repeat the emphasis of Benedict XVI, in his encyclical *Caritas in Veritate*, on nature as gift and Benedict's use of the phrase 'the grammar of nature':

> The human family has received from the Creator a common gift: nature. The Christian view of creation includes a positive judgement about the legitimacy of interventions on nature if these are meant to be beneficial and are performed responsibly, that is to say, by acknowledging the 'grammar' inscribed in nature and by wisely using resources for the benefit of all, with respect for the beauty, finality and usefulness of every living being and its place in the ecosystem. Nature, in a word, is at our disposition and we are called to exercise a responsible stewardship over it.

In paragraph nine of that message Francis pointed out that we are failing in the task of stewardship: 'So often we are driven by greed and by the arrogance of dominion, possession, manipulation and exploitation; we do not preserve nature; nor do we respect it or consider it a gracious gift which we must care for and set at the service of our brothers and sisters, including future generations.'

In an address at the University of Molise on 5 July 2014, Pope Francis insisted that 'one of the greatest challenges of our time [is] changing to a form of development which seeks to respect creation'. He added: 'This is our sin: exploiting the land and not allowing it to give us what it has within it, with our help through cultivation.'

Francis came back to the issue of care for the earth in the address he gave to the representatives of the people's movements at their gathering in Rome on 28 October 2014. The theme of that meeting was 'Land, Housing [literally, *techo*, 'a roof'], and Work.' The Pope said to them:

> There cannot be land, there cannot be housing, there cannot be work if we do not have peace and if we destroy the planet. These are such important topics that the peoples of the world and their popular organisations cannot fail to debate them. This cannot just remain in the hands of political leaders. All peoples of the earth, all men and women of good will – all of us must raise our voices in defence of these two precious gifts: peace and nature or 'Sister Mother Earth' as St Francis of Assisi called her.

He pointed out that an economic system which has at its centre the god of money makes it necessary also to plunder nature, in order to sustain the frenetic pattern of consumption which is an intrinsic aspect of the system.

He went on to say: 'Climate change, loss of biodiversity, and deforestation are already having the catastrophic effects which we are seeing; and it is you, the poor people who live in precarious dwellings near coasts, or who are so economically vulnerable, you are the ones who lose everything when a disaster strikes.' He insisted that creation is not an item of property that we can dispose of as we wish, still less a property owned or controlled by just a few people. On the contrary, it is a wonderful gift from God, entrusted to us to take care of and to use for the benefit of all. He concluded his speech by promising his listeners that he would take account of their concerns about these issues in his forthcoming encyclical.

Chapter Thirteen

A Different Kind of Development

When Francis calls for a change in the present model of development, he is taking up once again his critique of the present dominant system that does so much damage to poor and fragile people and to the fragile environment. His outspoken protest against this type of so-called development – and of the unrestrained capitalism on which it is based – finds strong support in the powerful polemic of Naomi Klein's book *This Changes Everything: Capitalism vs. The Climate*, and the extensive research and documentation that she cites. She maintains that 'there is a close correlation between low wages and high emissions' (Klein 2014, 81). She points out that 'we have not done the things that are necessary to lower emissions because these things fundamentally conflict with unregulated capitalism … [and] are extremely threatening to an elite minority that has a stranglehold over our economy, our political process, and most of our major media outlets' (Klein 2014, 18). Robert Manne (2015) shrewdly notes that Francis' position has much in common with that of Naomi Klein, but 'while the revolution Klein looks for is political and economic … the revolution that Francis' vision requires is cultural and spiritual.'

On 6 and 7 May 2015, Pope Francis and the Vatican endorsed a petition of the Global Catholic Climate Movement calling on world leaders to 'keep the global temperature rise below the

dangerous threshold of 1.5°C, and to aid the world's poorest
people in coping with climate change impacts'.

In his homily at the Mass for the opening of the Caritas
Internationalis General Assembly, 12 May 2015, Pope Francis
said:

> We must ... remind the powerful of the earth that God
> will call them to judgement one day, and it will be seen
> if they truly tried to provide food for him [Jesus] in every
> person, and if they worked so that the environment would
> not be destroyed, but could produce this food.

In an address to the participants of the meeting of the Food
and Agriculture Organisation (FAO) on 11 June 2015, Francis
pointed to a serious imbalance or injustice that has emerged in
recent times in the use of many agricultural products. Instead of
being used to meet the basic need of poor people for food, they
are instead being used to produce biofuels or to feed animals.

The increased emphasis of Francis on respect for the
environment was reflected in various Vatican-based agencies.
For instance, on 2–6 May 2014, an important joint workshop of
the Pontifical Academy of Sciences and the Pontifical Academy
of Social Sciences was held in the Vatican, under the title
'Sustainable Humanity, Sustainable Nature: Our Responsibility'.
In his opening address to this conference, Cardinal Maradiaga
said: 'Only through universal unitedness between men, animals,
plants, and things will we be able to push aside the conceit of
our race – which has come to think of itself as the despotic ruler
of Creation – and turn it into the elder brother of all of its fellow

creatures.' The final statement of the conference included this sentence: 'Today we need a relationship of mutual benefit: true values should permeate the economy and respect for Creation should promote human dignity and well-being.'

On 21 September 2014, the Interfaith Climate Summit held in New York issued a strong statement that was signed by representatives of a wide range of representatives from the religions of the world, including Cardinal Maradiaga (representing Caritas Internationalis) and Fr Michael Czerny, SJ (representing the Pontifical Council for Justice and Peace). The statement included the following words:

> As representatives from different faith and religious traditions, we … acknowledge the overwhelming scientific evidence that climate change is human-induced … When those who have done the least to cause climate change are the ones hardest hit, it becomes an issue of injustice … We recognise that climate change stands today as a major obstacle to the eradication of poverty.

The signatories went on to insist that the burden of limiting global warming to well below 2°c should be distributed 'in an equitable way'.

On 28 April 2015, Pope Francis met with UN Secretary General Ban Ki-moon before a summit conference of religious, political, and business leaders, scientists, and development practitioners held in the Vatican, under the title 'Protect the Earth, Dignify Humanity: The Moral Dimensions of Climate Change and Sustainable Development'. The aim of the conference was to 'build a consensus that the values of sustainable development cohere with values of the leading religious traditions, with a special focus on the most vulnerable'. Opening the conference, Ban Ki-moon said: 'The reason I am coming to the Pope is that now I need moral support.' The final declaration of the conference said:

> Human-induced climate change is a scientific reality, and its decisive mitigation is a moral and religious imperative for humanity. In this core moral space, the world's religions play a very vital role. These traditions all affirm ... the beauty, wonder, and inherent goodness of the natural world, and appreciate that it is a precious gift entrusted to our common care, making it our moral duty to respect rather than ravage the garden that is our home. The poor and excluded face dire threats from climate disruptions, including the increased frequency of droughts, extreme storms, heat waves, and rising sea levels.

In his various statements and comments in the period leading up to the promulgation of his encyclical on the ecology, Francis suggested that his understanding of the term 'human ecology' is subtly but significantly different from that of John Paul II and Benedict XVI. Rather than making a sharp contrast between 'human ecology' and 'natural ecology', he made a very close link on several occasions between exploited people and the exploited environment, describing both of them as 'fragile' or 'defenceless' (cf. *EG*, 56, 215). He did not set humans over against the rest of the natural environment. Instead, he used the term 'human ecology', mainly in terms of the responsibility of humans to protect creation in all its manifestations. This involves giving the term 'human ecology' a meaning similar to the way it is used in the social sciences. So it means that Pope Francis is situating us humans and our relationships within the context of our diverse social and cultural environments and, most especially, of our situation as an integral part of the whole evolving natural order.

Chapter Fourteen

An Encyclical on the Care of the Earth

Almost certainly the most important contribution by Pope Francis to Catholic teaching is a document called *Laudato Si'*, which is dated 24 May 2015 and was officially published on 18 June 2015. It is a 'papal encyclical', which means that it carries a high authority on an issue of official Catholic teaching. This encyclical of Pope Francis is the tenth in a series of 'social encyclicals' issued by various popes over the past one hundred and twenty-five years, each of which sets out the Church's teaching on various aspects of economic, political, social, and (more recently) ecological issues.

In giving the title *Laudato Si'* to the encyclical, Francis broke with tradition. Instead of giving it a Latin title, as is customary in official Vatican documents, he chose to take his title from the words of the eight-hundred-year-old 'Canticle of the Sun' written in medieval Italian by St Francis of Assisi: 'Praised be to you, my Lord.'

This encyclical is the first fully comprehensive treatment by a pope of environmental issues. So the subtitle of the document is 'On Care for our Common Home'. Perhaps a better English translation of the subtitle would have referred to 'our *shared* home' (rather than 'our *common* home') since its main thesis is that the earth on which we humans live is a home that we *share* with the other creatures of this world.

The encyclical locates humans as an integral part of nature and calls for what Francis terms 'an integral ecology'. The document is original both in its content and in its style. In it Francis enters into dialogue with other Christians, with people of other religions, with humanists, scientists, and politicians – inviting and challenging people everywhere to share his broad perspective on the role of humans in care for the earth and all its inhabitants. The encyclical shows that Francis has the courage to be controversial and challenging while maintaining a respectful and irenic posture.

HIS SOURCES

I begin by noting a point that makes this document quite different in style from all the great encyclicals issued by previous popes. This concerns the *sources* that Francis has drawn on. Whereas earlier popes had mostly quoted the documents of previous popes, Francis quotes from the environmental documents and reflections published by conferences of bishops from Bolivia, Brazil, Paraguay, Mexico, Argentina, Dominican Republic, the United States, Canada, South Africa, Australia, New Zealand, Japan, Germany and Portugal. In doing so he shows that he has not forgotten his commitment to exercising a collegial style of government and teaching in the Church, rather than having everything handed down from the Vatican. He takes account particularly of the documents issued by Church leaders who have been addressing real-life justice and ecological problems 'on the ground' in their particular regions.

He goes further by drawing also on the work of non-Catholics. In fact in the opening section of his encyclical, Francis quotes five different passages from a variety of statements of the Orthodox Patriarch Bartholomew (*LS*, 8, 9). This is highly unusual in a Vatican document and is a clear indication both of Francis' commitment to Church unity and his conviction that the pope and the whole Catholic Church have much to learn from other Christians.

Even more unusual and radical is the fact that Francis quotes the words of a Sufi mystic, the ninth-century Muslim poet Ali al-Khawas (cf. *LS*, 159). In this way Francis underlines his respect for other religions and his belief that religious people of all persuasions need to work together on issues of ecology and justice (cf. *LS*, 201). Furthermore, in sharp contrast to previous Vatican statements, he praises the work of the worldwide ecological movement (cf. *LS*, 14), in which leading roles are played by people who have little or no time for formal religion. At one point in the encyclical he quotes from what he calls 'the courageous challenge' of the *Earth Charter*, a document which some people would consider to be non-religious (*LS*, 207).

MISTREATMENT OF 'OUR COMMON HOME'

It is fairly widely known that in the first draft of the encyclical, which was prepared by a team under the direction of Cardinal Peter Turkson of Ghana, the first chapter was devoted to a scriptural theology of creation. But Francis has changed the order of the material. Being a Jesuit himself, he follows the pattern of the book called *The Spiritual Exercises*, written by St Ignatius Loyola, who was the founder of the Jesuit order. This book starts with meditations on our sinfulness. So, before describing a biblical ecological spirituality, and before spelling out what is involved in an ecological conversion, Francis invites us first to reflect on the sinful way we are despoiling and neglecting our world.

Already in the introductory paragraphs of the encyclical he reminds us of 'the violence in our hearts, wounded by sin', which has led us to harm 'our Sister, Mother Earth' 'by our irresponsible use and abuse of the goods with which God has endowed her' (*LS*, 1, 2). Then, in the first full chapter he puts forward a detailed account of the damage we humans are doing to the earth. In this chapter Francis outlines the different environmental problems that we face.

The account given by Francis of the ecological dangers which face our world is solidly based on the consensus view of the great majority of reputable scientists. Fritjof Capra notes that 'throughout the document, Pope Francis uses contemporary scientific language with complete ease' (Capra 2015). The success of Francis in accurately reflecting the consensus of scientists on climate change is due to the fact that leading scientists and ecological activists helped in the drafting of the document. One of them was Hans Joachim Schellnhuber, one of the world's leading climate scientists, who shared the platform in the Vatican at the launching of the encyclical.

Francis spells out the problems caused by climate change due to *global warming*. These include melting glaciers, rising sea levels, acidification of the oceans, and extreme weather events such as droughts and floods (*LS*, 23–8). While acknowledging that some environmental changes are caused naturally, he does not hesitate to challenge the climate-change deniers and sceptics, insisting that human activity is the main cause of the problems.

He goes on to point out that it is the poorest people who suffer most from these problems (*LS*, 48) even though they are the ones who have done the least to cause the problems.

There is also a lengthy account of a second major environmental issue, namely, *pollution* of indoor and outdoor air, of the land, fresh water, and the oceans (*LS*, 20–42). Francis says:

> Each year hundreds of millions of tons of waste are generated, much of it non-biodegradable, highly toxic and radioactive, from homes and businesses, from construction and demolition sites, from clinical, electronic and industrial sources. The earth, our home, is beginning to look more and more like an immense pile of filth. (*LS*, 21)

Closely related to the issue of pollution is the problem of waste. This is an ecological problem not only because of the pollution it causes but also because it involves using up the precious resources of the earth at an unsustainable rate. Francis says: 'The pace of consumption, waste and environmental change has so stretched the planet's capacity that our contemporary lifestyle, unsustainable as it is, can only precipitate catastrophes, such as those which even now periodically occur in different areas of the world' (*LS*, 161).

Francis makes an important distinction between two very different ways of handling 'waste'. On the one hand there is the kind of recycling that is part of natural ecosystems. This involves what is sometimes called a 'circular' model in which materials which are unused and rejected by one creature or process are absorbed and reused by other creatures or processes; one thinks, for instance, of how the dead bodies of animals and humans decay and are recycled by nature to provide nourishment for a whole variety of insects and plants. This contrasts sharply with what happens in almost all of our modern industrial systems. As the encyclical says, this 'has not developed the capacity to absorb and reuse waste and by-products. We have not yet managed to adopt a circular model of production capable of preserving resources for present and future generations' (LS, 22).

Francis is particularly concerned about the generation of waste by rich countries and rich people. He points out that 'approximately a third of all food produced is discarded, and … whenever food is thrown out it is as if it were stolen from the table of the poor' (LS, 50). So he protests against the present consumerist 'use and throw away' practice which generates so much waste (LS, 123).

The fourth problem that is treated extensively in the encyclical is the *loss of biodiversity* (LS, 24, 32–42, 167, 169, 190, 195). Francis maintains that a major cause of this loss is the modern mentality that sees the animals and the plants simply as resources, there to be exploited (LS, 33).

Loss of biodiversity involves not just a huge reduction in the number of elephants, tigers, polar bears, bees, and many other animals, insects, and plants. It means the elimination of whole *species* of creatures. For instance, it has been estimated that in the past fifty years, half of all the *kinds* of creatures in the oceans have been wiped out. Each of these species has had a history as long as our own human history and pre-history. Each developed in a unique way in response to the environment in which it existed. Each of them praised God in its own way by its very existence. The loss of each of these species leaves an irreplaceable gap in the symphony of creation.

What makes all this even more serious is that the way our ancient forests are being cut down, and the way our ocean fishing is carried out, means that we are wiping out whole species of creatures that we never even recognised. We are acting like people, who knowing nothing about art, barge into an art gallery and mindlessly destroy precious works without any awareness of the damage they are doing.

A central theme of the encyclical is the insistence by Francis that concern for the environment and concern for the poorest in our world are intimately linked. He repeatedly emphasises the point that the damage we are doing to the environment affects poor people most severely. He calls on us to 'hear both the cry of the earth and the cry of the poor' (*LS*, 49). So he takes a stand alongside the many campaigners for eco-justice, insisting that we must integrate justice into environmental discussions.

Chapter Fifteen

A Contemplative Spirituality

In a particularly important paragraph towards the end of the encyclical, Francis says that the ecological crisis is a summons to 'profound interior conversion'. He goes on at once to add:

> It must be said that some committed and prayerful Christians, with the excuse of realism and pragmatism, tend to ridicule expressions of concern for the environment. Others are passive; they choose not to change their habits and thus become inconsistent. So what they all need is an *'ecological conversion,'* whereby the effects of their encounter with Jesus Christ become evident in their relationship with the world around them. (*LS*, 217, emphasis added)

The ecological conversion for which Francis is calling gives rise to an ecological spirituality (cf. *LS*, 216) which has a contemplative component and an active component. Leaving over to later chapters the active aspect of this spirituality, this chapter focuses on the contemplative side. Francis is inviting us to immerse ourselves in a form of nature-mysticism (cf. Michaelson 2015). This is a quite radical alternative to the activism that is characteristic of Western society – and even of some of Western Christian spirituality. It involves being fully present to nature, to the scenery and the seasons, to the lilies of the field and the birds of the air (*LS*, 226). A contemplative approach enables us to 'be serenely present to each reality' (*LS*, 222) – including, of course, to each person with whom we come into contact.

In the introductory section of the encyclical, Francis reminds us that he took St Francis of Assisi as his 'guide and inspiration' when he was elected Bishop of Rome (*LS*, 10). When he describes the relationship that St Francis had with nature, he says that it is just like 'when we fall in love with someone' (*LS*, 11). The attitude of being in love with every aspect of the natural world lies at the very heart of the quasi-mystical kind of ecological spirituality that Francis is advocating. It is clear that he realises that it is love that will inspire and impel us to change our ecological behaviour, whereas guilt is a poor motivator – it often causes us to bury our heads in the sand.

So the Pope is inviting us to have a loving, intimate and tender relationship with the creatures and the world around us. He wants us not to approach them in a confrontational way, trying to squeeze them dry (*LS*, 106). We should rather see them as gifts: 'Creation can only be understood as a gift from the outstretched hand of the Father of all' (*LS*, 76; cf. *LS*, 5, 71, 146, 155, 159, 220, 226, 227).

For Francis, a key phrase is 'everything is connected' (*LS*, 91, 117; cf. 'everything is interconnected', *LS*, 70). Ecological activists express this idea by referring to 'the web of life' and the wider 'web of the cosmos'. We are an integral part of the web of life and of the cosmos; our bodies are composed of molecules that are billions of years old; and when we die these are 'recycled' into other parts of the web. The point of this image of a web is that when one touches any part of a web, this has a ripple effect which extends to every part of the web.

Francis does not use this image of a web; instead he uses the word 'network' which conveys the same idea (*LS*, 20, 134, 138). He also speaks of 'a loving awareness that we are not disconnected from the rest of creatures, but joined in a splendid universal communion' (*LS*, 220). The word 'splendid' is particularly appropriate since it suggests that the communion is not merely superlative but also has the quality of being marvellous and even mysterious, more than we can fully comprehend.

Francis draws a parallel between how we treat nature and how we treat humans: 'A sense of deep communion with the rest of nature cannot be real if our hearts lack tenderness, compassion and concern for our fellow human beings' (*LS*, 91). Later in the encyclical he says: 'We are speaking of an attitude of the heart, one which approaches life with serene attentiveness, which is capable of being fully present to someone without thinking of what comes next' (*LS*, 226).

MYSTICISM AND TRANSCENDENCE

The distinctive type of nature-mysticism favoured by Francis involves two levels of transcendence. In the first level of transcendence we recover 'a capacity for wonder which takes us to a deeper understanding of life' (*LS*, 225). This sense of wonder enriches, deepens, and even transforms our spirituality. It leads us into a deep gratitude and softens our hearts:

This conversion calls for a number of attitudes which together foster a spirit of generous care, full of tenderness.

> First, it entails gratitude and gratuitousness, a recognition
> that the world is God's loving gift, and that we are called
> quietly to imitate his generosity in self-sacrifice and good
> works. (*LS*, 220)

Francis goes on to say: 'As believers, we do not look at the world
from without but from within, conscious of the bonds with
which the Father has linked us to all beings' (*LS*, 220).

In the mystical spirituality of Francis, the first level of
transcendence involves experiencing nature in all its aspects
– animals, plants, scenery, weather, stars, and people – as
wonderful gifts from God. This enables us to find ourselves in
'serene harmony with creation'. And the result is that we are no
longer clogged up by 'frenetic activity' (*LS*, 225), by busyness and
the 'constant flood of new consumer goods [which] can baffle
the heart and prevent us from cherishing each thing and each
moment' (*LS*, 222; cf. *LS*, 113). This brings about a liberation
from worries and calculations about the future or the past. It is
an attitude which is beautifully expressed by Jesus in his advice:
'Do not worry, saying, "What shall we eat?" or "What shall we
drink?" or "What shall we wear?"' (Mt 6: 31). Francis points out
that it is related to a mentality adopted by those who 'take up an
ancient lesson, found in different religious traditions and also in
the Bible ... the conviction that "less is more"' (*LS*, 222).

The second level of transcendence brings us deeper. It comes
when we not only experience creatures as gifts of God but also
experience God in the gifts. So our contact with the people and the
non-human creatures around us become a means or channel for
coming in touch with God. Pope Francis says: 'The ideal is not

only to pass from the exterior to the interior to discover the action of God in the soul, but also to discover God in all things' (*LS*, 233).

This statement can be seen as an invitation to shift the focus of mysticism from the traditional approach which involved moving *inward* to one's spiritual depths; now we see that we can become mystics by moving *outward* to experience God in all of the creatures around us (I owe this point to a remark made by John Feehan in the course of an unpublished lecture). Of course these spatial images can be quite misleading when one is trying to describe the reality of mysticism; they exaggerate the contrast between the two approaches. The difference between the two is mainly a matter of a difference in one's starting point.

We experience each creature as an occasion for raising our voices with St Francis of Assisi in praise both of the creatures around us as gifts from God and of God, the ultimate Other whom we dimly experience *in* and *through* these gifts of nature. Pope Francis quotes from the 'Canticle of St Francis': 'Praised be you, my Lord, with all your creatures ... through Sister Moon and the stars, and *through* the air, cloudy and serene, and every kind of weather' (*LS*, 87, emphasis added).

Francis quotes St Thomas Aquinas, who wrote that God's goodness 'could not be represented fittingly by any one creature' so God created many creatures in order that 'what was wanting to one in the representation of the divine goodness might be supplied by another' (*LS*, 86). Each of these creatures by its very existence reflects some aspect of the reality of God – and in doing so it can be said to give praise to God. In the encyclical, Francis reminds us that we humans are not the only ones who praise God. Other parts of nature are so close to us, so similar to us, that they too can be seen as praising God in their own way. He says: 'The Psalms ... also invite other creatures to join us in this praise: "Praise him, sun and moon, praise him, all you shining stars! Praise him, you highest heavens, and you waters above the heavens! Let them praise the name of the Lord"' (*LS*, 72).

THEOLOGICAL BASIS

Francis provides us with a solid theological underpinning for the particular contemplative nature-mystical spirituality which he is advocating. He quotes St Bonaventure, a privileged follower of Francis of Assisi, who invites us to 'encounter God in creatures outside ourselves' (*LS*, 233). Invoking the Sufi mystic Ali al-Khawas, Francis also says: 'The universe unfolds in God, who fills it completely' (*LS*, 233). And to remind us even in this contemplative moment of the inseparable link between the fragile earth and fragile people, he immediately goes on to maintain that 'there is a mystical meaning to be found [not only] in a leaf, in a mountain trail, in a dewdrop, [but also] in a poor person's face' (*LS*, 233).

In a section of the encyclical with the significant title 'The Mystery of the Universe', Francis is careful to point out that he is not a pantheist. He says: 'Judaeo-Christian thought demythologised nature. While continuing to admire its grandeur and immensity, it no longer saw nature as divine' (*LS*, 78; cf. *LS*, 90). However, while insisting that creation is not God, Francis goes on to say that we can think of the whole of our universe 'as open to God's transcendence, within which it develops' (*LS*, 79). These words should be taken in conjunction with the following two sentences from the next paragraph:

God is intimately present to each being, without impinging on the autonomy of his creature, and this gives rise to the rightful autonomy of earthly affairs. His divine presence, which ensures the subsistence and growth of each being, 'continues the work of creation.' (*LS*, 80)[1]

Francis goes on to quote with approval the statement of the bishops of Brazil that 'nature as a whole not only manifests God but is also a locus of his presence. The Spirit of life dwells in every living creature' (*LS*, 88).

The technical term *panentheism* is not used in the encyclical. But when taken together, several short passages from paragraphs seventy-nine, eighty and eighty-eight add up to a position that is effectively panentheistic. This is the belief that God is present in every aspect of the creation, while not being identical with it. As a theological belief, it provides a strong basis for the special kind of nature-mysticism to which Francis is inviting us as a crucial aspect of an ecological conversion.

Prior to the coming of Francis, the Vatican was critical of 'certain ecological movements' on the grounds that they divinised the earth. Francis has not allowed this kind of suspicion to inhibit him from offering us a spirituality and theology that fully respects both the transcendence of God and, at the same time, God's immanence in our universe.

INTEGRAL ECOLOGY

Francis insists that concern for the environment is central to the

---

1 Each of these two sentences is backed by an endnote reference to the works of Thomas Aquinas.

Christian faith; it is 'not an optional or a secondary aspect of our Christian experience' (*LS*, 217). This is the fundamental basis for an ecological conversion. As a way of giving expression to what such a conversion involves, he puts forward his concept of 'an integral ecology', which for him is a key term. Pope John Paul II and Pope Benedict XVI were both inclined at times to put the emphasis on the *difference* between humans and other creatures, setting 'human ecology' over against a so-called 'physical ecology' or 'natural ecology' (cf. John Paul's encyclical *Centesimus Annus*, 38). Francis, by contrast, highlights all that we humans have in common with the rest of creation. He says, for instance: 'A good part of our genetic code is shared by many living beings ... Nature cannot be regarded as something separate from ourselves or as a mere setting in which we live. We are part of nature, included in it' (*LS*, 138–9).

The term 'integral ecology' is used eight times in the course of the encyclical (*LS*, 10, 11, 62, 124, 137, 156, 159, 225, 230). One important aspect of Francis' understanding of this term is that it represents a move away from the anthropocentric (human-centred) thrust of Catholic social teaching during the period from Vatican II up to the coming of Pope Francis in 2013. In Catholic teaching up to the time of Francis, non-human creatures were almost invariably seen as valuable primarily in terms of their use for humans.[2] A crucial aspect of the theological change represented by *Laudato Si'* is the insistence by Francis that non-human creatures have value in their own right; they have *intrinsic* value (*LS*, 33; cf. *LS*, 69, 115, 118, 140, 190). This

---

2 In an exception to this, we should note a passage from the *Catechism of the Catholic Church* which Francis quotes in endnote 43: 'Each of the various creatures, willed in its own being, reflects in its own way a ray of God's infinite wisdom and goodness.'

point is so important for Francis that he expresses it at times in language that is quite poetic. For instance, he says that even the smallest and most fleeting of creatures is enfolded in God's protection (*LS*, 77) and he even dares to say that 'everything is, as it were, a caress of God' (*LS*, 84).

Use of the term 'integral ecology' offers Francis a creative way of avoiding an explicit disagreement with the previous popes. Like them, he uses the term 'human ecology', but for him it generally has a different connotation – one could almost say a different meaning – because it is situated within the wider context of an integral ecology. It refers to our responsibility for all aspects of our lives – political, social, economic and cultural – and with particular reference to how our actions and whole way of life affects the earth. It is not surprising then that Fritjof Capra says that 'integral ecology', as used by the Pope, is equivalent to 'systems thinking' (Capra 2015).

The term 'integral ecology' has the further advantage that it is broad enough to cover within its wide ambit the protection of the unborn, which was a major concern of Pope Benedict when he used the term 'human ecology'. Francis expresses this eloquently:

> Since everything is interrelated, concern for the protection of nature is also incompatible with the justification of abortion. How can we genuinely teach the importance of concern for other vulnerable beings, however troublesome or inconvenient they may be, if we fail to protect a human embryo, even when its presence is uncomfortable and creates difficulties? (*LS*, 120; cf. *LS*, 117)

SACRAMENTAL SPIRITUALITY

Yet another advantage of the term 'integral ecology' is that it enables one to appreciate the ecological dimension of Catholic sacramental theology: 'The sacraments are a privileged way in which nature is taken up by God to become a means of mediating supernatural life … Water, oil, fire and colours are taken up in all their symbolic power and incorporated in our act of praise' (*LS*, 235).

Francis goes on to elaborate on this in some detail in his account of the Eucharist, which he says is the high point of all that has been created. He points out that Jesus comes to us 'not from above, but from within, he comes that we might find him in this world of ours' (*LS*, 235).

The point that Francis is making here is that the presence of Jesus in the Eucharist is an extension of the Incarnation of Jesus so to speak. We can spell this out more fully by recalling that Jesus took on our flesh, being born of a human mother and having a body composed of the same material as ours – the 'star-stuff' that emerged from the 'Big Bang' billions of years ago. Similarly, the material of the Eucharist is the material of our everyday world. As Sean McDonagh says: the bread and wine 'represent crops and vineyards, sunshine and rain, the God given bounty of the earth'. And they combine 'the fertility of the earth … with human creativity, in farming, baking, cultivation of vines and wine-making' (McDonagh 2016, 118, 120). So Francis says that 'Eucharist is itself an act of cosmic love … a source of light and motivation for our concerns for the environment, directing us to be stewards of all creation' (*LS*, 236).

Francis goes on to lay particular emphasis on the celebration of Eucharist on a Sunday, because every Sunday 'is meant to be a day which heals our relationships with God, with ourselves, with others and with the world'. The Sabbath, he says, is a day of rest which incorporates into our Christian spirituality the values of relaxation, festivity, 'receptivity, and gratuity'. In this way it 'protects human action from becoming empty activism ... and motivates us to greater concern for nature and the poor' (*LS*, 237).

Chapter Sixteen

The Biblical Foundation for an Ecological Conversion

So far I have been describing the contemplative dimension of an ecological spirituality. But this spirituality also has a more active dimension. This too is the fruit of the ecological conversion for which Pope Francis is calling.

Francis provides the biblical basis for this active aspect of the conversion by looking at key texts in the Book of Genesis (*LS*, 67). He responds to 'the charge that Judaeo-Christian thinking, on the basis of the Genesis account which grants man "dominion" over the earth (cf. Gen 1:28), has encouraged the unbridled exploitation of nature.' He says bluntly: 'This is not a correct interpretation of the Bible as understood by the Church.' He immediately goes on to add: 'Although it is true that we Christians have at times incorrectly interpreted the Scriptures, nowadays we must forcefully reject the notion that our being created in God's image and given dominion over the earth justifies absolute domination over other creatures.'

A little later he says: 'It would also be mistaken to view other living beings as mere objects subjected to arbitrary human domination' (*LS*, 82). In a subsequent chapter of the encyclical he says: 'Modernity has been marked by an excessive anthropocentrism.' Francis acknowledges that 'an inadequate presentation of Christian anthropology gave rise to a false understanding of the relationship between human beings and the world. Often, what was handed on was a Promethean vision of mastery over the world' (*LS*, 116).

Determined to correct this mistaken notion, Francis puts forward what he sees as the biblical basis for humans to have a 'correct' relationship with the rest of nature:

> They tell us to 'till and keep' the garden of the world (cf. Gen 2:15). 'Tilling' refers to cultivating, ploughing, or working, while 'keeping' means caring, protecting, overseeing and preserving.[1] This implies a relationship of mutual responsibility between human beings and nature. Each community can take from the bounty of the earth whatever it needs for subsistence, but it also has the duty to protect the earth and to ensure its fruitfulness for coming generations. (*LS*, 67)

The encyclical goes on to point out that the sabbath is a key element in an authentic biblical ecology. It says, 'Rest on the seventh day is meant not only for human beings, but also so "that your ox and your donkey may have rest" (Ex 23:12)' (*LS*, 68). Francis strongly rejects what he calls a 'tyrannical anthropocentrism unconcerned for other creatures' (*LS*, 68). He cites biblical passages that insist that humans should allow animals and land to have a sabbath rest and even to protect a bird that is caring for its chicks. He insists that the weekly

---

[1] It is interesting to note the similarity between this passage in the encyclical and some lines from a poem called 'Tragic Error' written many years earlier by Denise Levertov: '*subdue* was the false, the misplaced word in the story ... Surely our task was to have been to love the earth, to *dress and keep it* like Eden's garden' (Levertov, 1993, 62).

sabbath, the sabbatical year, and the Jubilee year have a twofold objective. Their purpose is, on the one hand, to ensure balance and fairness in the relationships between the human inhabitants and the land on which they lived and worked, and, on the other hand, to acknowledge that 'the gift of the earth with its fruits belongs to everyone; those who tilled and kept the land were obliged to share its fruits, especially with the poor, with widows, orphans and foreigners in their midst' (*LS*, 71).

Moving on to the New Testament, Francis says that Jesus was attentive to the beauty of the world and was constantly in touch with nature, 'lending it an attention full of fondness and wonder'. He often stopped to contemplate its beauty, and he invited his disciples to see a divine message in the fields, the seeds, and everything around them (*LS*, 97). In the next paragraph Francis went on to say that Jesus lived in such full harmony with nature that his followers were amazed to see that even the winds and the sea obey him (cf. Mt 8:27).

The encyclical then stresses the fact that Jesus worked with his hands. He was in daily contact with the matter created by God, and shaped it by his craftsmanship. In this way he sanctified human labour and endowed it with a special significance for human development. Francis notes that Jesus 'was far removed from philosophies which despised the body, matter and the things of the world'. And he adds regretfully that after the time of Jesus, some Christian thinkers disfigured the Gospel because they were infected by unhealthy dualisms of this kind (cf. *LS*, 98).

Then Francis reminds us that from the beginning of the world the mystery of Christ, the Word of God, has been at work in a hidden manner in the natural world as a whole, without thereby impinging on its autonomy. 'The destiny of all creation is bound up with the mystery of Christ, present from the beginning: "All things have been created though him and for him" (Col 1:16).' Then, quoting from the prologue to John's Gospel, Francis notes that this Word of God 'became flesh' (Jn 1:14) and threw in his lot with us humans (*LS*, 99).

Chapter Seventeen

Conversion of Culture

Building on this solid scriptural base, Francis spells out the practical implications of the ecological conversion that can lead to a truly integral ecology. For him, an ecological conversion is first of all a *personal* spiritual change in people 'whereby the effects of their encounter with Jesus Christ become evident in their relationship with the world around them' (*LS*, 217). But he goes on to say, 'The ecological conversion needed to bring about lasting change is also a *community* conversion' (*LS*, 219).

A large part of the encyclical is devoted to describing how the community dimension of an ecological conversion should be given expression or embodied in the economic, political, social, cultural and educational institutions of our world. I propose first to focus on the cultural aspect because it underpins the other aspects of the transformation involved in a comprehensive and integral ecological conversion.

Francis reminds us that 'culture is … a living, dynamic and participatory present reality, which cannot be excluded as we rethink the relationship between human beings and the environment' (*LS*, 143). He acknowledges the various ways in which technology has enabled humans to live more comfortably and has contributed to human artistic achievements (*LS*, 103). But he goes on to speak out strongly against what he sees as the fundamental mistake of most of the people who exercise power in our world. The term he uses to describe this mistake is 'the technocratic paradigm'.

THE TECHNOCRATIC PARADIGM

Almost all of the encyclical is written in quite simple language with very few technical terms. The most striking exception is the repeated use by Francis of the term 'the technocratic paradigm'. I suspect that many readers might go blank when they see these words. As a result they may miss one of the most important insights of Francis and one of the most important warnings that he is putting before us. So it is important to spell out what he means by this technical term.

When Francis refers to a technocratic paradigm, what he has in mind is a particular way of looking at reality, a reductionist mindset which causes us to interpret everything around and within us from a certain limited perspective. We then base our actions only on this incomplete viewpoint – one that is imperfect because it is incomplete. Francis says that 'humanity has taken up technology and its development *according to an undifferentiated and one-dimensional paradigm*' (*LS*, 106). He maintains that the basic mistake made by so many today is that they look at the world solely with the attitude and perspective of engineers or technical experts whose aim is to gain control over nature and use it for their own benefit.

Francis acknowledges that, over the centuries, humans have intervened and made changes in the world around them. In the past, however, 'this meant being in tune with and respecting the possibilities offered by the things themselves. It was a matter of receiving what nature itself allowed, as if from its own hand. Now, by contrast, we are the ones to lay our hands on things, attempting to extract everything possible from them while frequently ignoring or forgetting the reality in front of us.' He adds that this means looking at nature as though it were 'something formless, completely open to manipulation' (*LS*, 106).

A crucial element in this technocratic paradigm is the anthropocentric (human-centred) mindset which is central to most modern concepts of development. The world is seen entirely in terms of what benefits *humans* can draw from it. There is a failure to acknowledge the intrinsic value of non-human realities – animals, plants, forests or scenery.

Francis holds that a variety of serious problems spring from seeing and treating nature exclusively or mainly in this way. Firstly, it means that people 'no longer extend a friendly hand' to other people or to the animals, the plants, and all the other aspects of nature that are around us. Instead they relate to people and to other creatures in a confrontational way, seeking only to control them for their own benefit. Francis holds that this attitude is adopted particularly by economists, financiers and experts in technology. Their aim is to manipulate nature rather than to respect it and to be in tune with it.

This leads on to the second problem. Those who approach the world with such a mindset can easily assume that modern technology gives them unlimited power to solve all environmental and social problems through further technological inventions. Their single-minded commitment to controlling and exploiting nature leads them to take little or no account of the fact that there are limits to the resources of the earth. Quoting from the *Compendium of the Social Doctrine of the Church*, Francis speaks of 'the false notion that "an infinite quantity of energy and resources are available, that it is possible to renew them quickly, and that the negative effects of the exploitation of the natural order can be easily absorbed".' (*LS*, 106) There is an assumption that environmental problems caused by the present model of so-called development will be solved by future technological inventions.

At the heart of this problem is the fact that *development* is identified with *growth* and that it is assumed that technological advances always lead to *progress*. It is assumed that the only way to achieve ongoing human development is to make sure that the economy keeps on growing. And of course the use of the word 'growth' is itself quite misleading. What mainstream economists, planners, and politicians count as 'growth' of the economy fails to take account of much of the most important work that is done by people, including care in the home of children and older people, and huge amounts of voluntary work carried out in the community or at the national or global level. What is even more misleading is that much of what is called 'production' is actually closer to exploitation and consumption. Those who drill for oil or mine for coal are not actually producing anything; rather they are using up the resources of the earth.

A further problem is that the technocratic mindset 'ends up conditioning lifestyles and shaping social possibilities along the lines dictated by the interests of certain powerful groups' (*LS*, 107). So it is not just that technological control of nature is being used to exploit nature for the benefit of humans. It is that the benefits go almost exclusively to the so-called 'elite' – a relatively small number of wealthy and powerful people and nations –

while a very large proportion of the population of the world is left in poverty and deprivation.

And what do the privileged ones do with all this extra wealth? Do they use it to help those who have been left behind? Hardly ever. For the most part they allow themselves to get trapped in an endless spiral of buying unnecessary goods – thus adding to the ever-growing piles of waste. Towards the end of the encyclical Francis brings out the link between unchecked materialism and the technological paradigm. He says:

> Since the market tends to promote extreme consumerism in an effort to sell its products, people can easily get caught up in a whirlwind of needless buying and spending. Compulsive consumerism is one example of how the techno-economic paradigm affects individuals. (*LS*, 203)

Note his reference to 'the market'. A key point here is that the mindset which gives technological control of the world such a central place also leads to the production of a surfeit of unnecessary luxury goods. The economic system is such that if these goods are not sold, the *market* may collapse. This could quickly lead to an impoverishment of the people in power, so they dare not let it happen. For them the market has become an unquestionable 'power' – effectively a god. And in order to feed that ever-hungry god, a huge advertising and marketing industry has grown up. This is what leads to the consumerism which is so damaging to people and to the environment.

Francis dares to challenge that whole system in which 'the economy accepts every advance in technology with a view to profit, without concern for its potentially negative impact on human beings. Finance overwhelms the real economy.' This happens because groups whose only interest is in maximising profits have no concern for 'better distribution of wealth, concern for the environment and the rights of future generations' (*LS*, 109). Later in the encyclical Francis puts forward an even stronger criticism of this mindset:

> Where profits alone count, there can be no thinking about ... the complexity of ecosystems which may be gravely upset by human intervention. Moreover, biodiversity is considered at most a deposit of economic resources available for exploitation. (*LS*, 190)

RESISTING THE SYSTEM

According to Francis, if we are to create a genuinely ecological culture we need to adopt an alternative 'distinctive way of looking at things, a way of thinking, policies, an educational programme, a lifestyle and a spirituality which together generate resistance to the assault of the technocratic paradigm' (*LS*, 111). He even goes so far as to borrow a notorious phrase from Mao Zedong when he writes that there is an 'urgent need for us to move forward in a bold cultural revolution' (*LS*, 114). A cultural transformation of this kind is the only way to counter 'the mindset of those who say: "Let us allow the invisible forces of the market to regulate the economy, and consider their impact on society and nature as collateral damage"' (*LS*, 123).

Alongside our efforts to bring about a shift from the technocratic mindset, we need to work for the protection of non-

Western cultures, which have managed to preserve a healthier, ecologically oriented culture. Francis insists that 'it is essential to show special care for indigenous communities and their cultural traditions' (*LS*, 146; cf. *LS*, 179). The whole question of employment and unemployment is, of course, a crucial economic issue. So Francis devotes several paragraphs to this topic, insisting strongly on the importance of safeguarding people's employment (*LS*, 124–9). However, it is important to note that Francis also sees work as a fundamental *cultural* issue. He maintains that a proper appreciation of the role and value of human work is an important element in the cultural change for which he is calling. This is because, 'Work is a necessity, part of the meaning of life on this earth, a path to growth, human development and personal fulfilment' (*LS*, 128).

Towards the end of the encyclical Francis notes a further important dimension to his understanding of work: 'Christian spirituality incorporates the value of relaxation and festivity … We are called to include in our work a dimension of receptivity and gratuity, which is quite different from mere inactivity' (*LS*, 237).

It is clear that, for Francis, the crucial element in an ecological conversion is a willingness to resist the present-day consumerist culture. Referring to those who adopt a simple lifestyle, he says, 'Even living on little, they can live a lot, above all when they cultivate other pleasures and find satisfaction in fraternal encounters, in service, in developing their gifts, in music and art, in contact with nature, in prayer' (*LS*, 223).

Furthermore, he emphasises the importance of the 'historic, artistic and cultural patrimony which is … a part of the shared identity of each place and a foundation upon which to build a habitable city' (*LS*, 143). He maintains that this patrimony is under threat from the technocratic mindset. So an important aspect of the ecological conversion that he calls for is a serious commitment to preserve and develop people's rich cultural heritage:

> If architecture reflects the spirit of an age, our megastructures and drab apartment blocks express the spirit of globalised technology, where a constant flood of new products coexists with a tedious monotony. Let us refuse to resign ourselves to this. (*LS*, 113)

We are being invited by Francis, not just to change our mentality and mindsets, but to find ways of embodying a new way of thinking, feeling, and valuing in our buildings and our cities. He quotes from his apostolic exhortation *Evangelii Gaudium*: 'How attractive are those cities which, even in their architectural design, are full of spaces which connect, relate and favour the recognition of others!' (*LS*, 152).

As though to ensure that his concern about the design of cities could not be dismissed as elitist, Francis goes on immediately to address the very practical issue of the transport systems in modern cities. He agrees with those who insist on 'the need to give priority to public transportation'. But he also points out that this will not be widely acceptable if people have to 'put up with undignified conditions due to crowding, inconvenience, infrequent service and lack of safety' (*LS*, 153).

EDUCATION

Culture is shaped to a considerable extent by the formal education system of schools, colleges and universities. Equally important is the more informal education which takes place through the media, as well as through religious services and Church-run programmes.

Francis lays particular emphasis on the educative role of the *family* in shaping young people's awareness of their relationship with the rest of the natural world, and inculcating the virtue of respect for the environment. Not surprisingly, then, Francis has a lot to say about the 'educational challenge' which is required if we are to avoid environmental disaster (*LS*, 202, 209). In a particularly valuable passage he says:

> Environmental education has broadened its goals. Whereas in the beginning it was mainly centred on scientific information, consciousness-raising and the prevention of environmental risks, it tends now to include a critique of the 'myths' of a modernity grounded in a utilitarian mindset (individualism, unlimited progress, competition, consumerism, the unregulated market). It seeks also to restore the various levels of ecological equilibrium, establishing harmony within ourselves, with others, with nature and other living creatures, and with God. Environmental education should facilitate making the leap towards the transcendent which gives ecological ethics its deepest meaning. (*LS*, 210)

For Francis, an important component in a genuine ecological education is helping people appreciate literature, poetry, art, and the beauty of nature. He says, 'By learning to see and appreciate beauty, we learn to reject self-interested pragmatism' (*LS*, 215). He also insists that the aim of education must be not merely to provide information but also to instil good habits, to cultivate sound virtues (cf. *LS*, 211). An ecologically oriented education is integral: it seeks to shape more enlightened and responsible ways of thinking, of feeling, and of behaving.

Chapter Eighteen

Ecological Economics

If individuals, communities, and whole societies adopt the transformed culture described by Pope Francis, then it becomes realistic to believe that the present-day, market-dominated economics can be replaced by a truly ecological economics or what Francis calls an 'economic ecology' (*LS*, 141). This involves a rejection of the 'deified market' (*LS*, 56), 'a magical conception of the market, which would suggest that problems can be solved simply by an increase in the profits of companies or individuals'. In the same paragraph he points out that, 'Where profits alone count, there can be no thinking about ... the complexity of ecosystems which may be gravely upset by human intervention.' In that situation, he adds, 'Biodiversity is considered at most a deposit of economic resources available for exploitation' (*LS*, 190).

An important account of what Francis sees as essential to an ecological economics comes in this passage:

> Environmental impact assessment should not come after the drawing up of a business proposition or the proposal of a particular policy, plan or programme. It should be part of the process from the beginning, and be carried out in a way which is interdisciplinary, transparent and free of all economic or political pressure. It should be linked to a study of working conditions and possible effects on people's

physical and mental health, on the local economy and on public safety. Economic returns can thus be forecast more realistically, taking into account potential scenarios and the eventual need for further investment to correct possible undesired effects. (*LS*, 183)

Another crucial aspect of the converted economics that Francis calls for is that it puts a high value on employment – ensuring that people are not put out of work (cf. *LS*, 51, 127, 129, 189, 192). He says, 'In order to continue providing employment, it is imperative to promote an economy which favours productive diversity and business creativity.' He points out that most of the peoples of the world are engaged in 'a great variety of small-scale food production systems ... using a modest amount of land and producing less waste, be it in small agricultural parcels, in orchards and gardens, hunting and wild harvesting or local fishing.' This type of economy provides adequate employment, whereas modern systems which seek economies of scale 'end up forcing smallholders to sell their land or to abandon their traditional crops' (*LS*, 129).

A further essential aspect of a renewed economics is the adoption of more ecologically respectful methods of production and consumption (cf. *LS*, 5, 23, 138, 191). So too is a great reduction in the amount of waste we generate and the way we deal with it (cf. *LS*, 44, 50, 51, 90, 129, 161). For instance, the encyclical refers to the possibility of 'developing an economy of waste disposal and recycling' (*LS*, 180).

Pope Francis leaves us in no doubt that his concept of a truly ecological economy is one that takes full account of the impact of present-day economic decisions on the future generations of people and other inhabitants of our world. He insists that 'the notion of the common good also extends to future generations' (*LS*, 159), and his concern for future generations is expressed in no fewer than eight other paragraphs of the encyclical (cf. *LS*, 22, 95, 109, 160, 162, 169, 190, 195).

BLUNT CHALLENGES BY FRANCIS

Francis makes three very strong statements that are probably the most challenging in the encyclical. The first is this passage:

> Given the insatiable and irresponsible growth produced over many decades, we need … to think of containing growth by setting some reasonable limits and even retracing our steps before it is too late. We know how unsustainable is the behaviour of those who constantly consume and destroy, while others are not yet able to live in a way worthy of their human dignity. That is why *the time has come to accept decreased growth in some parts of the world*, in order to provide resources for other places to experience healthy growth. (*LS*, 193, emphasis added)

Peadar Kirby points out the courage of Pope Francis in this passage: 'He chose the issue that constitutes the greatest heresy for all mainstream economists, that we have to begin questioning growth as the motor of our economies' (Kirby 2017, 130).

Equally important and equally challenging is the second blunt statement of Francis, which is:

> We know that technology based on the use of highly polluting fossil fuels – especially coal, but also oil and, to a lesser degree, gas – needs to be progressively replaced without delay. (*LS*, 165)

Nowadays, these two issues – the acceptance of the need to reduce economic growth and the need to phase out the use of fossil fuels – are emphasised time after time, not merely by ecological campaigners but also by the majority of responsible scientists who have studied these issues. And, unfortunately, they are issues that politicians in both the developed and the developing world are very slow and reluctant to face up to and act upon.

However, quite recently a major campaign advocating *divestment* from fossil fuels by companies, universities, and religious groups of all kinds has developed to a point where it has become a major player in the economic system of the world. Very many companies and agencies have committed themselves to taking their investments out of fossil fuel companies and investing instead in alternative energy companies, and this number is increasing rapidly. This has put serious pressure both on the coal, oil, and gas companies and also on the investment agencies who handle the investments of those who have signed up to the divestment campaign.

In November 2017, the Global Catholic Climate Movement (of which the Irish Church-sponsored development agency Trócaire is a key member) produced an invaluable guidebook or 'toolkit' for Catholic religious congregations and other Catholic institutions (such as colleges and universities) that are willing to undertake this divestment process. It adopts the 'see, judge, act' approach which has been part of the tradition of Catholic social teaching since the 1960s. It includes a selection of case studies of groups that have already taken action on divesting from fossil fuel companies and re-investing in alternative energy agencies. (See *Ethical Investments in an Era of Climate Change: A Guide to Reviewing Environmental and Social Governance of Catholic Investments.*)

'ECOLOGICAL DEBT'

A third strong statement of Francis poses an enormous challenge that the leaders of the developed countries have been most reluctant to accept:

> Inequity affects not only individuals but entire countries; it compels us to consider an ethics of international relations. A true '*ecological debt*' exists, particularly between the global north and south, connected to commercial imbalances with effects on the environment, and the disproportionate use of natural resources by certain countries over long periods of time. (*LS*, 51, emphasis added)

Francis goes into some detail on this issue of ecological debt. He refers to the loss by poor countries of valuable raw materials which are exported from the South to the North, to deforestation, and to the environmental damage done to poor countries through the mining of gold and copper, dumping of toxic wastes, and the lack of adequate controls on pollution by companies operating in the South. He also mentions the global warming caused by the excessive consumption in rich countries, which causes particular problems in the South, especially in Africa (cf. *LS*, 51). By way of driving home his challenge to the leaders of the rich countries, Francis goes on to say: 'The foreign debt of poor countries has become a way of controlling them, yet this is not the case where ecological debt is concerned' (*LS*, 52).

As part of the Paris Climate Agreement of December 2015, the wealthy 'developed' countries reaffirmed their commitment to the pre-existing plan to provide US$100 billion a year in aid to developing countries for actions on climate change adaptation and mitigation. In this way they could be said to be acknowledging the reality of an 'ecological debt'. But serious doubts remain about their willingness in practice to live up to this commitment.

GENETIC MODIFICATION (GM)

In this encyclical Francis also takes a stance on another important issue – one on which the Vatican had been quite ambivalent prior to the papacy of Francis. This is the issue of the use of genetic modification to increase the yield of a variety of major crops, including soya, and wheat. This business is mainly controlled by four very large multinational corporations. These companies generally practise what is called 'vertical integration'. This means that they have a dominant position in all the stages of the production of food, from the modification of the seed up to the selling of the processed food. The practice is that a particular company manufactures and sells a pest-control insecticide which is specifically designed to be effective for the particular seeds which this company is selling. So those who sow the modified seeds have to buy this particular insecticide.

Pope Francis acknowledges that 'no conclusive proof exists that GM cereals may be harmful to human beings' (*LS*, 134). But he takes the risk of stepping into this highly controversial issue – and does so by issuing a strong but carefully nuanced warning about its dangers. He says that 'the risks involved are not always due to the techniques used, but rather to their improper or excessive application' (*LS*, 133). To bring this out he refers to a statement issued in 2005, by the Episcopal Commission for Pastoral Concerns, in Argentina. Relying on statements like this, he warns that, 'In many places, following the introduction of these crops, productive land is concentrated in the hands of a few owners.' The result of this 'expansion of oligopolies' is that the more vulnerable small farmers are put out of business. Some of them become temporary hired labourers on the large estates owned by multinational companies. Others leave their home areas and come to live in poverty on the margins of the overgrown cities (*LS*, 131–5).

Francis goes on to point out another serious consequence of the monopoly on genetically modified food crops by just the few multinational corporations who control the production of the modified seeds. He says: 'The expansion of these crops has the effect of destroying the complex network of ecosystems, diminishing the diversity of production and affecting regional economies, now and in the future' (*LS*, 134). When he speaks of diminishing the diversity of production, Francis is referring to the danger associated with monoculture. Traditionally there have been very many different types of wheat, soya, and every other food product. This provides a safety net. For example, if one type of wheat becomes vulnerable to a serious disease, farmers can switch over to a different type of wheat. But the agribusiness multinationals concentrate on just one variety and all the other types are in danger of being lost. This creates a great vulnerability in the production of food.

Francis also notes a further danger – one which has become all too real in recent years. This is the introduction by the big companies of *infertile* seeds. The farmers who rely on these seeds would no longer be able to hold over some of each year's crop to be the seeds for the crop of the following year. They would be forced to buy their seeds each year from the companies; and the companies would then have the farmers at their mercy. They could increase the price of these seeds to a point where many farmers would be put out of business. So Francis maintains that the dependency of farmers 'would be aggravated were the production of infertile seeds to be considered; the effect would be to force farmers to purchase them from larger producers' (*LS*, 134).

ALTERNATIVE ECONOMICS

The encyclical has words of praise for 'cooperatives of small producers' who adopt less polluting means of production (*LS*, 112). Similarly, there are places where 'cooperatives are being developed to exploit renewable sources of energy which ensure local self-sufficiency and even the sale of surplus energy' (*LS*, 179). Francis sees these cooperatives as models of an alternative economy – an economy that does not follow the dominant ideology of subordinating ecological concerns to the making of short-term profit.

On the question of alternative forms of energy, Francis says, 'How could we not acknowledge the work of many scientists and engineers who have provided alternatives to make development sustainable?' (*LS*, 102). He also maintains that 'poor countries ... are ... bound to develop less polluting forms of energy production'. He points out that this 'will require the establishment of mechanisms and subsidies which allow developing countries access to technology transfer, technical assistance and financial resources'. He adds, 'To do so they require the help of countries which have experienced great growth at the cost of the ongoing pollution of the planet' (*LS*, 172).

Somewhat surprisingly, the encyclical does not refer in any detail to the various alternative energy sources. Having noted how developing countries can take advantage of 'abundant solar energy' (*LS*, 172), Francis does not mention wind power, tidal power, or thermal energy from deep within the earth.

The encyclical offers no support at all to those who maintain that nuclear energy is the solution to the issue of global warming. Furthermore, Francis does not even bother to mention the more bizarre technological 'solutions' that are sometimes proposed – for instance, shooting billions of reflectors into or above the atmosphere in order to lessen global warming, or sucking huge amounts of carbon out of the atmosphere. Presumably Francis would say that the advocacy by some influential people for such measures is a clear indication of the extent to which they are influenced by 'the technological paradigm', which he believes is so prevalent in our world.

In this regard one might guess that Francis, or somebody who helped him draft this part of the encyclical, had been reading a book written by Naomi Klein just a year earlier. In that book she argues quite convincingly that reliance on this kind of 'geoengineering' is not merely futile but is part of the problem rather than a solution (Klein 2014, 256–68). So it is not so surprising that she was invited to take part in the Vatican conference about the encyclical in early July 2015.

Chapter Nineteen

Ecological Politics

Francis is well aware that small-scale alternatives undertaken on a voluntary basis cannot, on their own, constitute the economic conversion that is required to safeguard the earth and its more vulnerable inhabitants. He sees an urgent need for decisive *political* action to eliminate abuses. So he says:

> Civil authorities have the right and duty to adopt clear and firm measures in support of small producers and differentiated production. To ensure economic freedom from which all can effectively benefit, restraints occasionally have to be imposed on those possessing greater resources and financial power. (*LS*, 129)

What Francis is referring to here is a practice that is often called 'freeloading'. What this means is that one or two individuals or companies or countries take advantage of all the others by not abiding by the commonly accepted rules. A particular company may increase its profits by allowing its workers to be grossly overworked or exposed to environmental hazards, or by causing serious damage to the local environment. Or a country may allow its banks to loosen their controls to a point where the country becomes a haven where drug smugglers and other criminals can lodge their money without fear of detection or penalties.

The practice of freeloading occurs at both the national and the international levels. Focusing first on the national level, Francis maintains that when any policy, plan, programme or business proposition is being drawn up, it is important that all the different stakeholders should be involved and should reach consensus. He insists that 'the local population should have a special place at the table; they are concerned about their own future and that of their children, and can consider goals transcending immediate economic interest' (LS, 183).

Adequate protection of the environment is an issue that goes beyond individual countries. So Francis believes that there is urgent need for *international* binding agreements. Otherwise there will be a continuation of the present situation where countries compete with each other in regard to which of them can get away with doing the least to prevent further global warming and more exploitation and more pollution. The encyclical points out that 'it is essential to devise stronger and more efficiently organised international institutions, with functionaries who are appointed fairly by agreement among national governments, and empowered to impose sanctions' (LS, 175).

Francis harshly criticises political leaders who fail to respond adequately to ecological problems. He maintains that this happens because 'there are too many special interests, and economic interests easily end up trumping the common good and manipulating information so that their own plans will not be affected' (LS, 54).

He does not mince his words when he points out that the UN conference on Sustainable Development in Rio in 2012 'issued a wide-ranging but *ineffectual* outcome document' (LS, 169, emphasis added). Perhaps the Pope saw himself as contributing to the agenda of the COP 21 Paris Climate Change Conference of December 2015 when he wrote the following passage:

> A global consensus is essential for confronting the deeper problems, which cannot be resolved by unilateral actions on the part of individual countries. Such a consensus could lead, for example, to planning a sustainable and diversified agriculture, developing renewable and less polluting forms of energy, encouraging a more efficient use of energy, promoting a better management of marine and forest resources, and ensuring universal access to drinking water.
> (*LS*, 164)

And it is widely accepted that his words did indeed contribute significantly to the pressure on the almost two hundred leaders and heads of government who gathered in Paris and signed up to major environmental commitments.

From his experience in Latin America the Pope knew how the poorest people suffer when the water supply is privatised. So his emphasis in the above quotation on the right to universal access to drinking water is particularly significant. Earlier in the encyclical he had said: 'Fresh drinking water is an issue of primary importance, since it is indispensable for human life' (*LS*, 28). A little later he said: '*Access to safe drinkable water is a basic and universal human right, since it is essential to human survival and, as such, is a condition for the exercise of other human rights.* Our world has a grave social debt towards the poor who lack access to drinking water, because they are denied the right to a life consistent with their inalienable dignity' (*LS*, 30, emphasis in the original; cf. *LS*, 185).

We may presume that Francis is not suggesting here that the water supply must always be provided entirely free. It is more likely that what he is condemning here is a type of privatisation of the water supply that has occurred recently in some parts of Latin America – one where poor communities are left short of water because they are deprived of access to traditional sources of water, or because their area is not provided with an adequate water supply, or because the price is set at a level they cannot afford. The film *Even the Rain* vividly illustrates the problem.

By insisting on the universal right to clean water, Francis shows how aware he is of the need to protect 'the global commons'. This term refers to resources such as the oceans and the air, which are not confined to any one country. He says, 'What is needed, in effect, is an agreement on systems of governance for the whole range of so-called "global commons"' (*LS*, 174). The argument against the privatisation of commons is put forward very effectively by David Bollier (2014) who also emphasises the significance of new kinds of commons, such as Wikipedia and the Linux open-source software.

Francis adopts a controversial position when he puts forward a strong criticism of the system of 'carbon credits', which is widely used at present. He maintains that this arrangement appears at first sight to be an easy way for rich countries to avoid having to reduce their carbon emissions; but it is really a way of refusing to face the difficulty. It can give rise to speculation and actually enables rich countries and sectors of society to increase their carbon emissions (cf. *LS*, 171).

Responding to those who maintain that part of the solution to the environmental crisis is a reduction in the birth rate, Francis says bluntly: 'To blame population growth instead of extreme and selective consumerism on the part of some, is one way of refusing to face the issues. It is an attempt to legitimise the present model of distribution, where a minority believes that it has the right to consume in a way which can never be universalised, since the planet could not even contain the waste products of such consumption.' He does, however, qualify his statement by adding the rather vague comment that 'attention needs to be paid to imbalances in population density'(*LS*, 50).[1]

ACTION AT THE PERSONAL, SOCIAL AND COMMUNITY LEVELS

Francis is keenly aware that we dare not leave everything to the initiative (or lack thereof) of our political leaders. He holds that 'while the existing world order proves powerless to assume its responsibilities, local individuals and groups can make a real difference'. So he insists that 'society, through non-governmental organisations and intermediate groups, must put pressure on governments to develop more rigorous regulations, procedures and controls' (*LS*, 179). One of these non-governmental organisations is, of course, the Church. Francis says that all Christian communities have an important role to play in ecological education (*LS*, 214). This education can take place not only through words but also through a wide variety of committed actions.

---

1 See chapters twenty-one and twenty-four below for my comment on the position of Francis on the issue of population increase.

Pressure has to be put not only on governments but also more directly on business interests. Francis spells out one way in which this can be done. He points out that consumer movements bring healthy pressure to bear on those who wield political, economic, and social power by using the tactic of *boycotting* certain products. In this way, 'They prove successful in changing the way businesses operate, forcing them to consider their environmental footprint and their patterns of production' (*LS*, 206).

As I have already pointed out, Francis praises the cooperatives of small producers that model an alternative model of business that uses renewable sources of energy and fosters local self-sufficiency (cf. *LS*, 112, 179). He also recommends a whole series of practical actions that each of us can take: 'avoiding the use of plastic and paper, reducing water consumption, separating refuse, cooking only what can reasonably be consumed, showing care for other living beings, using public transport or car-pooling, planting trees, turning off unnecessary lights' (*LS*, 211).

TWO CONCLUDING PRAYERS

Drawing the encyclical to a close, Francis offers us two prayers that sum up the key themes of his encyclical. In the one which 'we can share with all who believe in a God who is the all-powerful Creator', he asks 'that we may protect the world and not prey on it' and that we may 'discover the worth of each thing, to be filled with awe and contemplation'. In the second prayer he addresses God as revealed to Christians: 'Triune Lord, wondrous community of infinite love, teach us to contemplate you in the beauty of the universe' (*LS*, 246).

ECOLOGICAL SPIRITUALITY

It is important to recognise that, for Francis, spirituality is not confined to just one item in his overall agenda. The whole of the *Laudato Si'* encyclical can be described as a call by Francis for us to adopt an ecological spirituality. I have already spelled out in some detail both the contemplative aspect of this spirituality and its action-oriented aspect. I have also noted the fairly brief treatment of the sacramental and liturgical dimension of the ecological spirituality that Francis is proposing (cf. *LS*, 235–7). So it suffices here to say that the main characteristics of the ecological spirituality in *Laudato Si'* are contemplative wonder, peace, joy, and hope combined with an active, passionate commitment by individuals, communities, the whole Church, and even (hopefully) whole nations and the entire global community, to protect the whole of creation, of which we are an integral part.

Chapter Twenty

A Spirituality of Deep Contemplation and Effective Action

In this chapter my aim is to summarise what I see as the major achievements of Francis in the encyclical *Laudato Si'*. It is widely accepted that it is an exceptionally important document. It will surely rank with the Vatican II document *Gaudium et Spes*, 'Pastoral Constitution on the Church in the Modern World'. I make this comparison because each of these documents represents a significant breakthrough in Catholic social teaching. Like *Gaudium et Spes*, *Laudato Si'* makes a major contribution, not just to the body of formal Catholic social teaching, but also to Catholic *spirituality*.

In *Laudato Si'* one does not find the suspicion with which the Vatican had tended in the past to view the ecological spirituality that had been emerging over the previous generation within the churches in other religions, and beyond the borders of all formal religion. It offers strong support for a contemplative and quasi-mystical spirituality.

AN ENRICHING CONTEMPLATIVE SPIRITUALITY
In this encyclical Francis invites us to take the time and leisure to really *experience* the trees, the animals, and the people which are all around us, as well as the scenery, the stars, and all the other wonders of nature. He suggests that our response should be, and generally

will be, one of wonder. This awe-filled experience of nature will, hopefully, induce us to a response of gratitude to the Creator for this abundance of gifts which we experience day by day.

However, Francis is not content with a spirituality which is centred on experiencing creatures as gifts of God. He invites us to go further. He suggests that at the core of our spirituality there can be an experience of God *in creation*. And he does this while in no way neglecting the transcendence of God.

AN ORIGINAL AND CHALLENGING ACTIVE SPIRITUALITY

The encyclical also contributes greatly to the active dimension of spirituality and to the enriched theology that underpins it. The main reason why Francis' account of an integral ecology is so significant is that he has moved beyond the anthropocentric (human-centred) approach of most previous official Vatican teaching. He recognises, firstly, that we humans are an intrinsic part of the cosmos and are close kin to other species. And, secondly, he insists that the other parts of creation have an intrinsic worth; their value does not depend solely on how they can serve human needs. In this way Francis provides a solid theological basis for a greatly enriched, actively committed Christian spirituality – one that is both personal and communal, including crucially important political and cultural dimensions.

At a practical level the encyclical includes many important developments in Catholic social teaching:

» It puts forward a rich Bible-based theology of ecology, which firmly rejects an anthropocentric interpretation of biblical texts that were used in the past to justify an exploitation of the earth's resources.

» It offers a comprehensive account of the major environmental issues facing our world in the present and near future, an account that is solidly based on the consensus of responsible scientists. Furthermore, this account is presented in a manner that the ordinary reader can understand.

» It maintains quite clearly that most of our environmental problems are the result of human actions and behaviour. So it poses a stern challenge to climate-change deniers and sceptics. Francis refuses to soften his stance on this issue despite serious pressure from some US think tanks, politicians and some prominent Catholics.

» In this encyclical Pope Francis insists even more strongly than he had done previously on the close linkage between concern for the fragile earth and for the most fragile people. He points out clearly and repeatedly that it is the poorest and most marginal people who suffer first and most seriously from environmental problems. It is in the light of this inseparable link that Francis calls on us to 'hear both the cry of the earth and the cry of the poor' (*LS*, 49).

» Francis maintains that most of our ecological problems are largely caused by what he calls the 'technocratic paradigm' that is dominant in our world today (*LS*, 101). He suggests that this mentality gives rise to the short-sighted, unsustainable, and exploitative style of so-called development, which has increasingly been adopted in almost every country of the world.

» He makes it quite clear that he is not simply repeating the traditional Catholic social teaching that criticises unregulated capitalism. He is challenging the specific type of business economics practised almost universally today and supported by most governments. So his position is quite close to that of moderate versions of liberation theology. This raises a serious challenge not just for the owners and managers of companies but also for politicians and for us, the citizens who elect our politicians.

» Francis issues a strong call for a search for an *alternative* economics – one that is based not on short-term profits but on concern for the common good of present and future generations of humans and of the other species with whom we share this world.

» In this regard, he has words of praise for local cooperatives and indigenous communities that are using environmentally friendly practices.

» He encourages initiatives by individuals and communities to adopt environmentally friendly practices. He challenges us to realise that quite radical changes are called for in our lifestyles: changes in our eating habits, transportation, generation of energy, and energy conservation.

» Nevertheless, he recognises that such small-scale efforts are not sufficient. So he insists on the need for enforcement measures at the national and international levels. This is the only way in which 'freeloading' industries or countries can be prevented from gaining unfair advantage over others.

» He supports the notion that politicians and business leaders should be pressured to take the radical enforcement actions that are required. This pressure can come from non-governmental organisations and from Christian communities. Francis goes further than previous popes in mentioning with approval the way consumer groups have succeeded in putting pressure on business interests by organising boycotts of certain products.

» The encyclical does not include the term 'restorative justice'. However, what Francis has to say about 'ecological debt' (*LS*, 51) amounts to a quite compelling case in favour of this kind of justice. He recognises that the better-off countries, mainly Western ones, have built their wealth to a large extent on their profligate use of the limited resources of the earth over the past two centuries – and on their mindless damage to the 'global commons' of oceans and air (*LS*, 174). Consequently, they are morally obliged to provide adequate support to poor countries in adopting a sustainable and ecologically respectful model of development through which they can overcome poverty. The passage in the encyclical on 'ecological debt' poses a serious challenge to the leaders and citizens of wealthy countries who are reluctant to acknowledge this kind of obligation – or at least to recognise the full extent of this 'debt'.

Chapter Twenty-One

Some Possible Improvements and Additions

There is so much that is truly valuable in the encyclical that I am reluctant to offer even any mild criticism of it. However, since I am attempting to provide a rounded assessment of this encyclical, I shall suggest some areas where I believe it might have been expanded and developed.

THE CONTEMPLATIVE ASPECT

On the contemplative aspect of the encyclical, I think it would have been helpful if Francis had taken the time to note how our relationship with trees, oceans, lakes, rivers, landscapes, and our gazing at sunsets or the moon or stars, all bring us nourishment and healing of body and spirit. This is very well brought out by John Feehan who bases it on our evolutionary history:

> It is … literally and scientifically quite true to say that we were made to live in an open space with abundant trees; we are genetically programmed for that. We cannot do without it … The places where Nature still breathes awake in us memories of a deeper childhood … We respond to trees … are most at home in their presence because this is where we were born, this is what we were made for. (Feehan 2016, 142–3)

Similarly, the poet Mary Oliver says: 'When I am among the trees … they give off such hints of gladness, I would almost say they save me, and daily' (Oliver, 123). This is the most primordial element in our experience of nature; it underpins our sense that the realities around us are gifts from the Creator.

The insistence by Francis that we can actually *experience God in* these gifts is such a crucial element in the spirituality of Francis that it deserves to be spelled out in more detail. A more elaborate treatment could throw more light on the fact that many people who have a truly deep ecological spirituality are still resistant or reluctant to say that what they feel is an experience of God. I venture to suggest that the issue here is not any lack of depth of these people's experience but rather the way in which most believers have trivialised God, glibly assuming that we know who or what God is.

Once again John Feehan comes to our rescue. For him, mysticism 'is, in essence, that small, still, wordless voice from without, heard from within' (Feehan 2015, 11). He points out that we learn from mystics like Meister Eckhart that, even though creation is suffused with God's presence, the immediacy of this experience cannot be adequately articulated or communicated in words (Feehan 2015, 14–15). Feehan reminds us that our awareness of God in nature is 'deeper than any conceptualisation can reach'. He goes on to say that 'any attempt to define it will cause it to retreat because, indeed, as the deepest spirituality in all the religious traditions reminds us, it is not to be named, is beyond name' (Feehan 2016, 90).

This suggests that ecologically aware Christians who believe we can experience God in nature need to be tentative and humble in making that claim. We dare not imagine that our experience is deeper than those who say that their spirituality has no need for God and no room for God. Their more implicit unarticulated experience of mystery, of depth, perhaps of a Beyond, may in fact be deeper and more authentic than ours. As Feehan points out, the presence of God 'is in the personal experience of the encounter, not in words'. So he maintains that the personal language of our Christian tradition is not the only language in which the invitation to come closer can be articulated. 'It might as easily have been the impersonal language of much eastern religion, or even a language that in the academic halls in which it echoes carries no mention of a godhead' (Feehan 2015, 20).

We might express the same view in a different way by making a clear distinction between faith and 'the faith'. Faith is the gift which invites and enables us to respond authentically in wonder, gratitude, and a sense of our own inadequacy, to the mystery in which we find ourselves. The phrase 'the faith' usually refers to the tentative and incomplete set of belief statements in which we partially succeed in articulating that response of ours. We need to be keenly aware that the unarticulated *faith* of a person who claims to be an 'unbeliever' may in fact be a more authentic faith than that of some Christians who confidently proclaim their explicit faith in God but whose actual experience of the Mystery whom we call God is lacking in depth. In such a situation God may be willing, and may perhaps even prefer, to remain anonymous.

EVOLUTION

In paragraph seventy-nine of the encyclical Francis speaks of 'things evolving positively'. In the following paragraph he says that the divine presence 'continues the work of creation'. And he adds: 'The Spirit of God has filled the universe with possibilities and therefore, from the very heart of things, something new can always emerge.' It is clear, then, that Francis is very aware that our universe is *continuing to evolve* and that the Spirit is continuing to preside over the ongoing process of evolution. However, the encyclical includes surprisingly little about the whole process of evolution.

Francis lays great stress on the fact that we humans are an intrinsic part of the great 'network' which includes the whole of creation (cf. *LS*, 134, 138). He reminds us that science has shown the extent to which we share much of our DNA with other creatures, even those that might have seemed quite different from us. He insists repeatedly that we live as part of a complex web of relationships with the rest of creation, which sustains our very existence. But in the encyclical he does not spell out *how* this has come about. John Feehan suggests that the reason why Francis says so little about evolution is probably that he did not want 'to stir up a hornet's nest of conservative outrage in the Church' (Feehan 2017, 66). If this is the case, one may admire the diplomacy of Francis. But it is nevertheless regrettable that he did not include a somewhat fuller treatment of evolution as the fundamental cause of how everything in our universe is linked to everything else.

Modern scientific advances have enabled us to look back in time to the instant of the primordial explosion 13.75 billion years ago when our universe began. We are beginning to understand how, from that starting point, there emerged a universe of ever-increasing complexity. Ilia Delio, drawing on the work of Niels Henrik Gregersen, points out that 'nature is a nested hierarchy of ontological levels'. What this means is that new higher-level realities emerge, composed of lower-level components. The nature and functioning of each new level of reality cannot be understood or predicted on the basis of our knowledge of the lower-level constituent parts. For instance the science of physics cannot adequately 'explain' what happens at the chemical level; the behaviour of animals cannot be fully explained by use of chemical science; and the distinctive features of what it means to be human cannot be adequately explained in terms of animal psychology. As Delio says, 'the whole is greater than the sum of its parts' (Delio 2011, 54–5).

This evolutionary emergence did not, and does not, take place in any deterministic fashion. Apparently random interactions and statistical probabilities are central to the process. Nevertheless, one can discern in these interactions a certain upward-directed intentionality that Bernard Lonergan has helpfully described as 'emergent probability' (cf. Lonergan 1992, 145–6).[1]

In the English text of *Laudato Si'* there is one phrase that seems rather odd: 'even if we postulate a process of evolution' (*LS*, 81). This wording seems to suggest that there is real doubt about the reality of evolution – and it is very unlikely that this was the intention of Francis. The context suggests that in using these words he is referring not to evolution in general but to

---

1 For an insightful account of how this differs from deterministic versions of Darwinism, and how it expands and corrects Darwin's own work, see Byrne 2009, 13–57, especially 36 and 51–3.

the specific issue of the evolution of *humans*. So I think a better phrasing would have been to replace the word 'if' with the word 'though'. The passage would then read, 'even *though* we accept that there is a process of evolution'.

In regard to the emergence of humanity Francis repeats the traditional Catholic insistence that this required 'a direct action by God'. I venture to suggest that this is an unnecessary and outdated way of expressing a vital truth. The kernel of the Catholic belief is that humans are qualitatively different from their non-human ancestors. As Christians, we believe that God is the primary cause of the whole process of evolution, including the emergence of humans. God's action is transcendent in its nature. To make a distinction between 'direct action' by God and indirect action is to apply categories that are applicable *within* our universe. It is unnecessary and inappropriate to use the words 'direct' and 'indirect' to God's transcendent causal action. We do not need to speak of a direct action by God in relation to humanity in general or to each human person. It suffices to say that humans in general are unique in our world, and that each human person is unique – and that all this is part of the creative plan of God, which unfolds in the process of evolution.

'THE NEW STORY'

Our growing understanding of this process of evolution has enabled theologians, following the inspiration of Teilhard de Chardin, to develop what the pioneering Passionist priest and self-styled 'ecologian' Thomas Berry has called 'The New Story'. This New Story of creation supplements and enriches the biblical 'Genesis Story' of creation and the elaborate Bible-based theology on which Christians have relied until recent times.

It does so by taking seriously the story of the evolutionary process as revealed by the scientists, seeing the world as 'a continuing process of emergence in which there is an inner organic bond of descent of each reality from an earlier reality' (Berry 1978, 6). One must then go on to appreciate the fact that 'the universe carries within it a psychic as well as a physical dimension'. 'Each new level of being emerges through the urgency of self-transcendence' and if this were absent, human consciousness would emerge 'out of nowhere' and would find 'no real place in the story' (Berry 1978, 8).

The *spirituality* that emerges from this understanding has two key aspects. The first is that we can have 'confidence in the *continuing revelation* that takes place in and through the earth' (Berry 1978, 13).[2] The second aspect is that we now have 'a new paradigm of what it is to be human' – an awareness that humans, having emerged through the earth's process, are now largely responsible for how that process develops (Berry 1978, 9).

Some Church leaders and theologians (including some ecologically minded ones) have reservations about the term 'The New Story'. This is mainly because some enthusiasts for this approach have suggested that it replaces the traditional theology of Christ and redemption. Another mistake is the assumption by some that the adoption of 'The New Story' dispenses one from the need to engage in serious dialogue with scientists on the nature of the whole evolutionary process – a process that the

---

2 I have emphasised the words 'continuing revelation' to recall that the encyclical uses this phrase in *LS*, 85.

scientists themselves are only gradually coming to understand. Needless to say, Thomas Berry himself cannot be held responsible for these unfortunate distortions. And it would be a pity to dismiss his rich insights and the term 'The New Story' simply because of the mistakes of some of his would-be 'disciples'.

Although Francis refers in one endnote to Teilhard de Chardin, he does not refer to Thomas Berry and does not make any explicit reference to 'The New Story'. I think that a serious lack in the encyclical is its failure to give an account of this new theology and spirituality. Francis may have felt it was wiser not to use the term 'The New Story' because under previous popes the Vatican had been quite mistrustful of ecological theology and of the spirituality associated with this term. But there is no doubt that the theology and spirituality that Francis advocates coincide to a considerable extent with that of the New Story.

I think it would have added greatly to the comprehensiveness of the encyclical if Francis had referred more extensively to how our theology and spirituality can be enriched by taking more account of the reality of evolution as revealed by modern science. I think especially that the contemplative quasi-mystical spirituality that Francis puts forward would be greatly enhanced if people were encouraged to experience wonder and awe in the face of the complexity and beauty not just of the multiform creatures in our world but also of the process of evolution through which they have emerged. The New Story approach could inspire people to think poetically of our universe as a cosmic symphony, which began with the extraordinary drumbeat of the Big Bang, which develops though many 'movements', and which is evolving towards a culmination that for us remains shrouded in mystery, but which our faith assures us is already anticipated in the resurrection of Jesus.

THE COSMIC DIMENSION OF THE INCARNATION

Francis quotes the Canadian bishops as saying that 'nature is … a continuing revelation of the divine' (*LS*, 85).[3] The phrase 'continuing revelation' can be understood as equivalent to the phrase 'primary revelation', which is now widely used in theology. What this phrase refers to is the fact that the revelation of the Jewish scriptures and of the New Testament follows on from, and in some sense presupposes, the revelation of God in creation, starting with the Big Bang of 13.75 billion years ago. As Leonardo Boff says, 'there cannot be a contradiction between the book of the world and the book of the scriptures' (Boff 1997, 151). When I use the word 'primary' in this context I mean simply that this aspect of revelation comes first *in time*; I am not suggesting that it is *more important* than the revelation in the Bible.

One way of expressing the importance of this 'primary revelation' is to speak of the 'Cosmic Christ'. Unfortunately, this is a phrase that remains obscure and misleading for many people. The main reason for the confusion is that people fail to realise that the word 'Christ' is a *title* that is given to Jesus; it is not exclusively a part of the *name* of Jesus. So the word 'Christ' can be applied not just to the historical Jesus but also to other aspects of the presence of the Word of God in creation. Those who use the phrase the 'Cosmic Christ' are emphasising

---

3 I note, however, that in his comment on the Canadian bishops' words, and again later in this paragraph, Francis himself uses the traditional word 'manifestation' rather than the word 'revelation'.

the point that billions of years before 'the Word was made flesh' in the person of Jesus, the Word of God had already become 'embodied', in a different way, in the natural world. Ilia Delio writes, 'The whole cosmos is incarnational' (Delio 2011, 50); and Richard Rohr (2011) says, 'The Christ is born the moment God decides to show himself ... The Big Bang is the birth of the Christ ... That's the Cosmic Christ.' He spells out the relationship between Jesus and 'The Christ':

> Jesus is the microcosmic expression of the macrocosm, the union of human and divine ... in a single life and person ... a concrete and personal embodiment of universal love ... The Christ includes and goes further than Jesus, beyond space and time. (Rohr 2017)

Personally, I am rather hesitant about using the phrase 'Cosmic Christ'. This is not because I disagree with the whole concept of a 'primary revelation' but simply because people are liable to be confused by the term 'Cosmic Christ'. I find it somewhat more helpful to speak of 'the cosmic dimension of the incarnation of the Word of God.'

A scriptural basis for the concept of a 'primary revelation of God in creation' can be found in the opening verses of St John's Gospel. It tells us that through the Word of God 'all things came into being'. The Word of God has been present and active in our universe from the first moment of its existence. The stars, the planets, the oceans, and the trees are 'manifestations' of the Word of God. And the word of God 'takes flesh' in some degree in the earliest humans and, in a lesser way, in the animals. Each in its own way reveals some aspect of the divinity. Some theologians express this reality by using the term 'Deep Incarnation'.

Margaret Daly-Denton writes a perceptive commentary on John's statement that through the Word, the *Logos*, 'all things came into being':

> From the idea that all things were created through the *Logos* it follows that everything in the creation was intended by God to be a revelation, a communication, a *logos* with a small 'l' so to speak, a word from God for human beings to hear, heed and reflect upon, thereby learning something about its source. (Daly-Denton 2017, 34)

Both Jews and Christians believe that the revelation of the Word finds more explicit expression in the Jewish scriptures. The distinctive feature of the Christian faith is that we believe that the revelation of the Word finds its high point and fulfilment in the person of Jesus.

However, we can now see more clearly that the coming of Jesus as the definitive Word of God was not just a disruptive intervention by God into a world in which God had previously been absent. The Gospels of Matthew and Luke tell us that he had a human ancestry stretching back for hundreds of years. And now we know that this implies that he also had a far longer pre-human ancestry, stretching back to the moment our universe came into being. Jesus as human is fully embedded in the history of our cosmos, which began 13.75 billion years ago.

An even fuller and more complete connection between the human Jesus and the wider cosmos comes through his

Resurrection. Key passages in the Epistles of Saint Paul (Col 1:12–20; Eph 1:3–10) assure us that the Resurrection of Jesus is the first step in the transforming restoration of the entire creation. As Denis Edwards puts it, in the Resurrection, 'Jesus of Nazareth becomes the Cosmic Christ' (Edwards 1999, 122). In the encyclical Francis says, 'The ultimate destiny of the universe is in the fullness of God, which has already been attained by the risen Christ' (*LS*, 83). At that point Francis adds a footnote in which he makes a rather vague and cautious reference to the contribution of Pierre Teilhard de Chardin, SJ (*LS*, footnote 53). As I suggested earlier, it might have been helpful if Francis had included, at least in that note, a mention of the contribution of Thomas Berry to our understanding of the cosmic aspect of the Incarnation.

THE ACTIVE ASPECT OF THE ENCYCLICAL

There are some topics where the treatment in the encyclical would have been more helpful and challenging if the subjects had been covered somewhat more extensively. For instance, Francis says: 'When media and the digital world become omnipresent, their influence can stop people from learning how to live wisely, to think deeply and to love generously' (*LS*, 47). However, it would have been helpful if he had gone on to mention that the media in very many countries are owned or controlled by a small number of extremely rich individuals or companies. These are generally a key part of the powerful establishment whose interests would be threatened if the readers and viewers knew the full facts of the situation.

Francis makes one oblique reference to the role of the advertising industry in creating a throwaway, wasteful, and ecologically damaging culture. He says that 'the market tends to promote extreme consumerism in an effort to sell its products' (*LS*, 203). But it would have been helpful if he had spelled out explicitly and bluntly the extraordinary power of the advertising industry, the huge sums of money that are spent on advertising, and the shocking extent to which it contributes to creating a consumerist and wasteful culture.

LIMITING POPULATION GROWTH

It is a pity that the treatment of the population issue in the encyclical is brief and incomplete. Pope Francis and his advisers were doubtless acutely aware that, if the encyclical had contained anything new or significant on the issue of population control, the mass media were likely to focus on this; so the main message of the encyclical could be missed. Furthermore, Francis might have wished to leave the topic of responsible parenthood – and the morally acceptable means to achieve it – to the Synod of Bishops in Rome which was scheduled to take place in October 2015. These considerations may help explain why he mentions the issue of population control only briefly.

The encyclical maintains that the extreme consumerism by wealthy people is the real problem (*LS*, 50; cf. R. Williams 2015). However, it would have been helpful if Francis had repeated in polite and measured terms the remarks he had made during his journey back to Rome from the Philippines on 19 January 2015. On that occasion he rejected the idea that 'in order to be good Catholics, we should be like rabbits' and used the phrase 'responsible parenthood' twice.

Francis could have strengthened his case for linking the issue of poverty with that of protecting the environment by pointing out why it is economically necessary and socially acceptable for poor people in developing countries to have large families. They have a high level of infant mortality and no public social security system. The children who survive are expected to support members of the immediate and extended family, especially their parents and relatives in their old age. The conclusion is obvious: the only effective way to avoid a population explosion in poor countries and at the same time to protect the environment is to develop an ecologically sustainable model of development that gives priority to the elimination of poverty and that provides people with some adequate level of social security.

We must acknowledge with Francis that wealthy individuals and nations put far more demands on the resources of the earth than poor people and poor nations do. But we must also acknowledge that the very rapid population growth in many poor countries is putting intolerable strain on the limited resources of these countries. The question that arises is what are the acceptable *means* for limiting population growth. If we rule out the use of abortion and compulsory sterilisation this leaves us with the issue of the use of contraceptives.

Francis has not given any indication that he envisages a repeal of the ban on the use of artificial contraception issued in 1968 by Paul VI in *Humanae Vitae*. However, it would have eased the consciences of many devoted Catholics if he had given an account of the difference between subjective and objective morality as well as the crucial importance of discernment – an account similar to the one he gave a year later in chapter eight of *Amoris Laetitia*. Furthermore, in response to a question on his flight back to Rome from Mexico on 17 February 2016, Francis said: 'The great Paul VI, in a difficult situation in Africa, allowed nuns to use a form of artificial contraception amid the violence. It is important not to confuse the evil of preventing pregnancy, in itself, with abortion.' This indicates that in his view it could be morally acceptable for a woman to use contraception to protect herself against rape or violence.

THE SITUATION OF WOMEN

One of the most important features of the encyclical is the way in which Francis emphasises time after time the close linkage between poverty and the environment, between fragile people and the fragile earth. It is now widely recognised that, in general, poor women are the poorest of the poor. In almost all poor countries there is a patriarchal system which gives men and boys a more privileged position than women and girls. It is regrettable that Francis did not speak out specifically against this reality when he was addressing the problem of poverty.

In an earlier chapter I noted the very strong stance which Francis has taken on the issue of human trafficking, which is a modern form of slavery. In *Laudato Si'* he makes several passing references to this crime against humanity (*LS*, 91, 123, 197). And we cannot doubt that he knows that women and girls are by far the greatest number of those who are trafficked for sexual exploitation. It would have been helpful if the encyclical had noted this reality and linked it to the wider issue of how women in our world are so often exploited and treated as second-class citizens.

ACTIVE RESISTANCE BY CHRISTIAN COMMUNITIES

In the encyclical Francis suggests that Christians – and especially Christian communities – can and should play an important role in campaigning for a more just and ecologically respectful model of human development (cf. *LS,* 179, 206, 214). However, I think it would have been very helpful if he had spelled this out rather more explicitly. He could have included in this encyclical some of the quite radical remarks which he had made to the *movimentos populares* in his two addresses to them – more particularly the one he gave in Bolivia on 9 July 2015 (see my treatment of this in chapter five). He might have encouraged Church leaders and Christians 'on the ground' to establish such active campaigning groups in every part of the world.

Chapter Twenty-Two

Follow-Up to the Encyclical

Francis continued to make important interventions on environmental issues even after *Laudato Si'* had been published. On 7 July 2015 during a trip to Latin America he spoke with educators in Quito. He said that God gives us creation as a gift, a present, an offering. 'It is not something that can be bought or acquired.' In his address to activists, in Santa Cruz de la Sierra in Bolivia (which I examined in some detail in chapter five) he asked them to take personal and community action to protect the environment: 'I ask you, in the name of God, to defend Mother Earth ... The future of humanity does not lie solely in the hands of great leaders, the great powers and the elites. It is fundamentally in the hands of peoples and in their ability to organise.'

One of Francis' more striking messages was issued on 18 July 2015, shortly after his return to Rome from that journey to Latin America. This was his message to participants in a conference in Rome organised by the Pontifical Council for Justice and Peace about the effects of mining in their countries. In this message he spelled out eloquently and in some detail the very damaging environmental and human costs of the manner in which mining takes place in many countries at present. He listed six 'cries' that are heard, including a cry of sadness and impotence for the contamination of water, air, and land, and a cry of indignation and for help for violations of human rights. He insisted that 'the entire mining sector is undoubtedly required to effect a radical paradigm change to improve the situation in many countries'.

In an address on 11 September 2015 to participants in a meeting in Rome on sustainable development he asked how we are to serve the common good by dealing with issues such as climate change. He answered this question by insisting that every individual is called to respond personally, with whatever responsibility that person has, whether in the family, or the workplace, or research, or the economy or in civil society. He pointed out that the solutions can only come through a joint effort. And we must avoid what he called 'the great enemy', the hypocrisy involved in making verbal commitments which are not acted on.

ADDRESSES TO THE US CONGRESS AND THE UNITED NATIONS

One of the more significant speeches that Francis gave during his visit to the United States was his address to the Joint Congress on 24 September 2015. In the course of this wide-ranging speech he devoted an important paragraph to recalling and quoting his appeal in *Laudato Si'* for 'a courageous and responsible effort to ... avert the most serious effects of the environmental deterioration caused by human activity.' He stressed the 'important role' that the United States and Congress can play on this issue. As always he linked care for the environment with care for vulnerable people, quoting from his encyclical: 'Now is the time for courageous actions and strategies, aimed at implementing a "culture of care" (*LS*, 231) and "an integrated approach to combating poverty, restoring dignity to the excluded, and at the same time protecting nature"' (*LS*, 139).

226

On the following day, 25 September 2015, Francis gave a major address to the members of the General Assembly of the United Nations. In it he put forward a comprehensive position, including a variety of topics such as sustainable development, the importance of peace-making, the damage done by drugs, respect for religious freedom, and the whole issue of human rights. Interestingly, one part of his speech was a close echo of a key part of his address to social activists in Bolivia on 9 July 2015; this was where he had said that everybody has a right to the 'absolute minimum ... lodging, labour, and land.'

The most original and striking element in his address to the UN was his stark statement: 'It must be stated that a true "right of the environment" does exist' (*'existe un verdadero "derecho del ambiente"'*). This raises an interesting challenge for theologians and philosophers. Their task is to explore and explain what it means for Francis to claim that the environment has rights. They may explore how his statement can be interpreted in terms of the human rights tradition, or the natural law tradition, or an ethics based on virtue or value.

It seems, however, that Francis was not unduly concerned with any such philosophical exploration. He simply went on immediately to give two reasons to justify his claim that 'a true "right of the environment" does exist':

First, because we human beings are part of the environment. We live in communion with it, since the environment itself entails ethical limits which human activity must acknowledge and respect ... Any harm done to the environment, therefore, is harm done to humanity. Second, because every creature, particularly a living creature, has an intrinsic value, in its existence, its life, its beauty and its interdependence with other creatures ... In all religions, the environment is a fundamental good.

In this way Francis finds the basis for his statement at the UN in what he had already said in *Laudato Si'* that 'everything is connected' (*LS*, 91, 117), in his insistence that non-human creatures have intrinsic value (*LS*, 33), and in his call to us to hear 'the cry of the earth' (*LS*, 49).

The argument of Pope Francis might be elaborated philosophically by noting that human rights and any other kind of rights must always be situated within a *network* of other rights, because every creature exists within this one universe of ours where everything is linked to everything else. And many of these rights are 'competing' with each other.

For this reason it is not enough for a moralist or anybody else to start a discussion about rights by simply declaring that one particular right or set of rights is absolute. No right comes with a ready-made label saying that it is an absolute right. It is true that we may and do decide to consider that certain rights must be respected by everybody and at all times. This is because the human community, on the basis of careful discernment, has come to recognise that these rights are so fundamental that we must treat them as inviolable. So we call them 'absolute rights' and defend them as such.

It is helpful to remember that Francis is not saying that each member of every species has an absolute right to exist. Not all rights are absolute. In this regard it might be better if the text of the Pope, or its English translation, had said that the non-human parts of creation have *inherent* value rather than *intrinsic* value. That is because the word 'intrinsic' might be understood to be equivalent to 'absolute', as when Church leaders and some moral theologians say that certain actions are 'intrinsically evil'.

The challenge facing all of us – and particularly our scientists, our planners and our politicians – is to determine the *extent* to which it is right and appropriate to modify our environment and use the resources of the earth for our benefit or according to our wishes. Can it ever be acceptable to keep chickens locked in narrow cages and fill them full of antibiotics? Is it ever acceptable to put a pet dog to death – and, if so, under what circumstances? When is it right to cut down a particular tree? These are questions to which there are no ready-made answers. Authentic answers can only emerge when wise people study all the circumstances and engage in respectful dialogue and careful personal and communal discernment.

A further point is that in the debate about rights it may be assumed that those who have rights are people who have the ability, at least in principle, to *claim* those rights. However, in the Catholic view and that of many others, infants in the womb and people who are entirely incapacitated by severe mental illness or mental disability still have fundamental rights, even though they cannot explicitly claim their rights. It is not such a radical step to move on from this to maintaining that animals and trees can also have rights. But I think we have to accept that the word 'right' is being used in a real but analogical sense when it is applied to animals, trees, and the environment as a whole.

Some moralists may prefer to remain within the natural law tradition rather than to situate themselves within the rights tradition. Those who take this position may interpret the words of Pope Francis about the right of the environment as being simply the equivalent of saying that we humans have a serious moral obligation to protect the environment, to care for the earth.

Next I quote an eloquent passage from the address of Pope Francis to leaders of the Pacific Islands Forum, on 11 November 2017. He spoke of 'the need for a global outlook, international cooperation and solidarity, and a shared strategy, which can prevent us from remaining indifferent in the face of grave problems such as the deterioration of the environment and of the health of the oceans, which is itself linked to the human and social deterioration experienced by humanity today.'

WITH THE AMANZONIAN PEOPLES

In the following years Francis continued to insist on many occasions on the importance of care for the earth. Not surprisingly, he gave what is probably his most forthright and radical statement on the topic when, on 19 January 2018 in Puerto Maldonado, Peru, he addressed thousands of members of more than twenty-three different indigenous peoples from several countries of the Pan-Amazonian region of Latin America. He said:

The native Amazonian peoples have probably never been so threatened on their own lands as they are at present. Amazonia is being disputed on various fronts. On the one hand, there is neo-extractivism and the pressure being exerted by great business interests that want to lay hands on its petroleum, gas, wood, gold and forms of agro-industrial monocultivation. On the other hand, its lands are being threatened by the distortion of certain policies aimed at the 'conservation' of nature without taking into account the men and women, specifically you, my Amazonian brothers and sisters, who inhabit it. ... We have to break with the historical paradigm that views Amazonia as an inexhaustible source of supplies for other countries without concern for its inhabitants.

Francis went on to refer to the practical problems faced by the indigenous peoples. He spoke of 'disturbing reports about the spread of certain diseases'. So he said: 'We call upon states to implement policies of intercultural health that take into account the experience and the worldview of the native people, training professionals from each ethnic group who can deal with the disease in the context of their own worldview.'

Francis made a particularly strong plea on behalf of those who are called 'Indigenous Peoples in Voluntary Isolation' (PIAV). These are the groups who have isolated themselves in the deepest heart of the Amazon forest in order to 'live in freedom' and protect their way of life by cutting themselves off from contact with the rest of the world. Francis spoke of them as 'the most vulnerable of the vulnerable'. Protesting against 'consumerist greed', he said that limits have to be set to ensure that their habitat is protected.

The Pope insisted that we need to appreciate the essential contribution that these peoples bring to society as a whole.

'Their cosmic vision and their wisdom have much to teach those of us who are not part of their culture.' Later in his address he said: 'The culture of our peoples is a sign of life. Amazonia is not only a reserve of biodiversity but also a cultural reserve that must be preserved in the face of the new forms of colonialism.'

What is particularly significant in this address is that it shows clearly the reason why Francis is so sharply critical of the utterly insensitive manner in which multinational companies treat the Amazon region simply as an economic resource to be exploited. He points out that the result of this exploitation is not just the mindless destruction of an irreplaceable ecological resource – the Amazon forest as one of the major 'lungs of the planet'. Equally, or even more important, is the insistence by Francis that protection of the environment is inextricably linked to the protection of *people* and of the diverse *cultures* in which people live.

Section Three

INTEGRAL SOCIAL TEACHING

Chapter Twenty-Three

Catholic Social Teaching Today

Pope Francis has contributed so much to Catholic social teaching that I think it may be helpful to devote this chapter to listing what I see as the many strong points in that teaching at the present time. In the following chapter I shall list a number of issues on which the Church's social teaching needs further development.

The first and greatest strength of the tradition of Catholic social teaching is that it has become truly *integral* to the issuing of *Laudato Si'*. Up to the time of Pope Francis, official Catholic teaching had a rather strong anthropocentric character. The *integral ecology* put forward by Pope Francis is no longer anthropocentric but situates us humans within our environment. The word 'ecology' as commonly used refers to nature as distinct from what is human. But the integral ecology of Francis is not confined to non-human nature. It also includes the whole range of what is involved for humans in being 'at home' – including culture, politics, and economics.

The second strength of the Church's social teaching is that it is truly *humanistic*. It is not, of course, humanist in the sense of excluding faith or the supernatural. In saying it is humanistic I am referring to the deeply human aspect which Pope John Paul II constantly emphasised, for instance, in his first encyclical

(*Redemptor Hominis*, 14–15), and in his centenary encyclical (*Centesimus Annus*, 53–5).

A particular advantage of having a social teaching that is both humanistic and ecological is that it aims to appeal not merely to Christians but to all people of goodwill. Furthermore, it means that there is room for a constant dialogue with other traditions – not merely a desire to teach others but also a willingness to *learn* from others. Perhaps the most obvious example of this is the way in which over the past generation the popes have taken up and used the language of human rights, which was originally articulated not in the Catholic tradition but in the humanistic traditions of Enlightenment France and the newly independent United States. More recently the Church has begun to make its own the moral wisdom that is emerging through the ecological movement and the feminist movement, neither of which was distinctively Catholic at first.

A third strength of Catholic social teaching is that it has a rich *contemplative* dimension. Prior to the coming of Francis, the contemplative aspect of social teaching was more or less implicit. But in *Laudato Si'* Francis insists strongly and eloquently that the Christian understanding of our close relationship with the rest of the natural world nourishes our spirits and can lead us into a contemplative quasi-mystical experience of solidarity, sisterhood/brotherhood, and even oneness.

The fourth strong point about the Church's social teaching is that it has a solid basis in the Bible. One of the most helpful parts of *Laudato Si'* is its section on the biblical basis for a theological ecology. The fact that Catholic social teaching on justice and ecology is soundly biblical means that there is ample room for ecumenical dialogue on social issues with other Christian churches, most of which tend to rely more on the Bible than on a natural law or humanistic basis.

A fifth strength of Catholic social teaching is that it is prophetic in the sense that it is radically challenging and inspirational. The ecological teaching of Francis provides a solid biblical-theological basis for a *prophetic* ecological spirituality, which is a profound and uncompromising challenge to the present dominant model of the unsustainable development that exploits both the earth and its poorest people.

The Church's prophetic teaching calls on settled people to open their hearts and their countries to refugees. It is uncompromising in its condemnation of the oppression and trafficking of people, of the exploitation of the earth, and of the consumerism and alienation linked to these abuses.

This teaching is in direct continuity with the words of the Old Testament prophets in denouncing injustice and announcing new hope for all, above all for the poor and oppressed, as well as in its insistence on respect for the land. At its best it can be experienced as a sharing in the liberating task of Jesus. It calls on Christians and all people of goodwill to work for a fundamental reshaping of society both at the global and the local levels.

Over the past fifty years Catholic social teaching has come to a deeper understanding of the Church's call to side with the poor and the powerless in working for justice and for respect for the environment. And it has found in the term 'preferential option for the poor and for the earth' a striking and effective way of expressing this call. For these reasons Catholic social teaching is inspiring and evangelical, a teaching which lies at the heart of the Christian faith.

A sixth strength of Catholic social teaching is its strong emphasis on solidarity and 'the common good'. When people take solidarity seriously it rescues them from selfish individualism and enables them to avoid the danger of an unduly individualistic conception of personal human rights. A sense of solidarity gives people an awareness that they are responsible for each other and for the welfare of the community. Solidarity is a virtue that gives people energy and even passion. So they are not content with theory and words. Rather they act justly in their personal lives and they work and struggle for justice and ecological respect both in the wider society and in any organisation or movement, including the Church, in which they are involved.

In more recent years, there has been a further development in relation to solidarity, namely a stronger insistence on the importance of intergenerational solidarity. In their teaching, both Pope Benedict and Pope Francis have emphasised our responsibility for future generations. So solidarity is to be extended in time as well as in space.

However, Francis has gone much further; he invites us to have a sense of *solidarity with other living beings* and with the whole of creation. This means that he has effectively extended the meaning of the term 'the common good' to include not just humans but also all the other creatures with whom we share this universe.

A further point is that its emphasis on the common good and on solidarity with all of humanity and with other creatures provides Catholic teaching with a solid basis for people to act responsibly in the sexual sphere. When people are liberated from a narrow and selfish individualism, they can freely choose how best to engage in loving sexual relationships. Being aware of the problem of overpopulation, fertile couples may choose responsibly to be loving with each other in ways that limit the number of their children. Couples who are biologically infertile may feel that they have a particular responsibility to extend their love for their partners to the wider local community and to the global community, human and non-human. The motivation of those who freely choose to be celibate may include a desire to exercise their love in a manner that does not burden our overstretched world with a larger human population than it can sustain.

There is one key point about the full understanding of 'the common good' as developed by Pope Francis. It is that he defends the approach which has come to be called 'the seamless garment' of respect for life. He strongly affirms the Church's unequivocal opposition to abortion. But he also firmly opposes capital punishment; and he teaches that it is immoral even to possess nuclear weapons, and that a non-violent struggle for justice should replace the older conception of a 'just war'. Furthermore, he calls us not merely to respect human life at all its stages but also to respect and protect the non-human living creatures who share our world.

A seventh strength of the Church's social teaching is the way in which it stresses the inseparable link between justice and ecology. This linkage was already present in the document 'Justice in the World', issued by the 1971 Synod of Bishops in Rome. Pope Francis has taken up this theme and made it central to his social teaching. His position is encapsulated in his insistence that at the heart of the Christian faith is a commitment to protect fragile people and the fragile earth – to hear the cry of the earth and the cry of the poor. One striking example of the link between justice and ecology is the fact that environmental problems in poorer countries are largely caused by the global warming generated mainly by richer countries. And these environmental problems in poor countries are a major cause of the huge increase in the number of economic migrants seeking asylum in the so-called 'developed' countries. Furthermore, there is a direct link between ecological problems in poor countries and the exponential growth in crime gangs engaged in the trafficking of people.

An eighth strength of Catholic social teaching is that it offers a profound and uncompromising challenge to the present dominant model of the unsustainable type of *development* that exploits both the earth and its poorest people. It does not limit itself to speaking out against unjust actions or people. Rather it condemns the sinful *structures* that are both the effect and the cause of acts and attitudes of social injustice. It goes some way toward identifying the historical, economic, and cultural root causes of global poverty and inequity.

A ninth strength of Catholic social teaching is its strong affirmation of personal human *rights*. Because the fundamental basis of Catholic teaching is respect for human dignity, it puts the focus not merely on political and civil rights but equally on social, economic, and cultural rights, such as the right to adequate housing, secure employment, and respect for cultural differences. Francis has expanded the concept of rights by extending it to include the environment. The natural law tradition and the human rights tradition can fit together very well and each can enrich the other and compensate for the weaknesses of the other tradition.

A tenth strong point of Catholic social teaching as it is understood today is that it focuses particular attention on the right to participation. This value is crucial because it puts limits on the arbitrary exercise of power by those in authority. In any society or organisation where the value of *participation* is respected, people themselves can claim their own rights and shape their own destiny. So participation is a value that opens the way to a wide range of other values. It serves to give content to Catholic social teaching in a variety of different situations, and it provides criteria that can be applied in practice. Furthermore, those who participate in decision-making are energised, feel respected, and have a sense of involvement and ownership in the whole project. In *Laudato Si'*, Pope Francis has put a strong emphasis on the need to ensure that the voices of all the stakeholders are heard on any development issue.

An eleventh important strength of Catholic social teaching is that it insists that it is essential to tackle not just absolute poverty but also relative poverty. This point was already made by Pius XII as long ago as 1941. But, as I suggested in chapter six, it is put in very stark terms by Pope Francis in his statement: 'Inequality is the root of social ills' (*EG,* 202).

A twelfth strength of Catholic social teaching is its emphasis on what Pope Benedict called an 'economy of communion'. By this term is meant a system in which the purpose of a business enterprise is defined as not just making profit for the owner or shareholders; its purpose also includes a commitment to benefit all the other 'stakeholders', including the workers, the suppliers, the buyers of the product, the local community, and the environment. If this approach were widely accepted it would go a long way towards 'humanising' the at present largely unrestrained capitalist system. However, the emphasis which Pope Benedict placed on the importance of 'an economy of communion' needs to be balanced by the strong emphasis which Pope Francis and previous popes placed on an overt struggle for justice and liberation.

The thirteenth strong point of the Church's social teaching is that it is compatible with a certain pluralism. It is open to a variety of applications on different continents, in different eras, and in different circumstances. Very closely related to this is the fact that, while touching on the political sphere in a general way, Catholic social teaching seeks to avoid being identified with the policies of any particular political party or movement. It claims rather to offer criteria by which such specific policies may be evaluated.

The official Church has learned how important it is to keep at a certain distance from the popular trends or preferred options of any particular era, even those which seemed very admirable to Christian leaders at the time. Around the time of Leo XIII it seemed to many that the true Christian option was a revival of the guild system. In the 1930s it seemed that a vocational or corporative organisation of society was the only correct Christian answer to social problems. After World War I and again after World War II there was a strong move to identify Church teaching with the policies of Christian Democratic parties in many countries. In the aftermath of John XXIII's encyclicals many Christians opted for a 'welfare state' model. In the late 1960s and early 1970s 'Christians for Socialism' and other New Left movements seemed to many to be the only authentic way forward. From the mid-1980s onward some sectors of the Church, especially in the United States, came to believe that the solution is to identify authentic Catholic social teaching with a close linkage between democracy and capitalism.

There have been occasions when various popes have flirted to some extent with one or other of these trends – but never to the extent to which the enthusiasts would have wished. On the whole, the popes and bishops have tried to keep the official Church above politics; they have maintained a certain distance from specific applications of the general principles, leaving it to lay Christians as citizens to opt for one policy or another. However, they have not hesitated to suggest that some of the proposed policies – particularly outright socialism and unrestricted capitalism – are incompatible with the basic principles of Catholic social teaching. The accusation that Pope Francis is a communist or a socialist is not justified. In fact there is a strong case for saying that Catholics who accuse him of being a communist have themselves fallen into the trap of believing that the capitalist system is the *only* valid Christian social and political system.

The final item on this list of strong points in Catholic social teaching may at first sight seem surprising. It is the clear distinction made by Pope Francis between, on the one hand, the *objective* teaching of the Church including its doctrines and its moral laws, and, on the other hand, *subjective* morality where the emphasis is on personal conscientious decisions. This distinction has of course always been a part of the Catholic tradition. But

243

Francis has applied it in practical pastoral situations far more clearly than in the past. As we saw in chapter two, he has done this most obviously in the area of sexual morality; but it also applies more widely to all issues of social morality.

The particular contribution of Francis on the question of subjective morality is his emphasis on the crucial importance of discernment. He brings out the point that this *discernment* has to take place not only at the purely personal level, but also jointly with the aid of a wise and experienced mentor; and he also stresses how important it is for whole communities to engage together in discernment on issues that are of common concern.

Chapter Twenty-Four

More to Do

Having listed the many strong points in current Catholic social teaching, I believe it is important to balance this by noting that there are several areas in which this teaching is somewhat weak, or at least insufficiently developed.

The first and most obvious inadequacy in the social teaching of the Catholic Church is its failure to provide an adequate treatment of the issue of justice for women. It is a matter of astonishment that in a world where women exercise top leadership roles in various governments, the business world, and the media, they are precluded from holding significant authority in the institutional (hierarchical) structures of the Catholic Church. This was understandable – though of course inexcusable – in the past when Catholic theology held that women were inferior to men and that 'the woman's place was in the home'. But in more recent years Church authorities – influenced, sometimes reluctantly and occasionally gratefully, by the widespread challenge to patriarchy – now affirm that women have an important contribution to make to public life.

In attempting to be true to the message and spirit of Jesus, official Catholic teaching has insisted time and time again over the past fifty years that women are equal in dignity and status to men. Church leaders have spoken out strongly against the many injustices suffered by women. One thinks particularly of the teaching and actions of Pope Francis on the issue of human trafficking, a major part of which involves the trafficking of women and girls for sexual exploitation. I would add that in view of the extraordinary increase in internet pornography in recent years, it would be good if Church authorities spoke out even more strongly than previously against this very serious abuse of women.

In light of the advances in Catholic teaching on the rights of women, it is a cause of serious disquiet, even of scandal, that Church authorities have not yet been prepared to allow women to hold leadership roles in the Church equivalent to those held by men. Pope Francis insists repeatedly that 'everything is connected' in our world and our cosmos. That women are not allowed to play their full part in the ecclesiastical sector of the interconnected web of life must be seen as a serious flaw in the web, one that mars its beauty and damages its effectiveness.

The Church must find a means of enabling women to play a central role in formulating the social teaching and policies of the Church, especially, but not exclusively, in the aspects that concern women. An important step in the right direction would be that the Vatican should at last act more effectively than in the past on the recommendation of the 1971 Synod of Bishops that a mixed commission be set up to explore the issue of the role of women in society and in the Church.

The question concerning the ordination of women is not identical to the issue of women being given fully authoritative roles in the Church. But the two issues are closely linked, and the exclusion of women from ordination seems to be used by Church authorities as an excuse for not facing up to the choice of appointing women to top leadership roles in the Vatican. So long as this anomaly remains in the practice of the Catholic Church, it remains as a fault line that seriously lessens the credibility of its teaching over the whole range of Catholic social teaching.

The ordination issue is hugely controversial. A significant number of responsible theologians and committed Catholics do not agree with the view of Pope Francis that Pope John Paul II gave a fully definitive decision that women cannot be ordained. Pope Francis established a commission to examine whether women were ordained as deacons in the early Church. If this commission gives the answer 'yes' to this question, then the issue of women being ordained to the priesthood will become even more controversial. We must hope that the commission will soon issue their report.

A second inadequacy in official Catholic teaching – even in *Laudato Si'* – is the absence of an explicit emphasis on the 'New Story'. This account of evolution provides the basis for a rich and comprehensive spirituality that appeals both to the head and to the heart. Catholic teaching on the environment would be greatly enriched if it took more account of this concept.

A third weakness of Catholic social teaching is that it does not yet provide us with practical criteria for discerning the limits of human interference with nature. Catholic teaching has not succeeded in giving us clear guidelines for knowing how to respect the integrity of creation. There is need for serious work to be done on the right to continued existence of various species of living beings and even of individual animals, as well as on the duty of humans to protect places of natural beauty.

A fourth weakness of Catholic social teaching is that the human values that it embodies may not be as fully transcultural as they have been assumed to be. These values were articulated almost entirely in the context of Western theology. Rome has been unduly reluctant to allow the local churches of different continents to develop their own articulations of social teaching. The present body of teaching, for all its merits, needs to be supplemented, and partially corrected, by the values that have been or will be articulated in situations where Christianity is incarnated in Asian, African, Oceanic, or Latin American cultures, as well as in the many subcultures in various parts of the world. An example may bring out the point. At present, Catholic social teaching seems generally to presuppose that the word 'family' refers to the nuclear family. Consequently, it tends to neglect or ignore the rich values embodied in the *extended family*, although this is an institution that plays a central role in the lives of most African peoples and many of the peoples of Asia and elsewhere.

Another example raises even more far-reaching questions. Catholic social teaching now places a lot of emphasis on the right to development. But it is essential to distinguish between development, on the one hand, and *Western-style* development, on the other. Many Church leaders and theologians have not succeeded in holding on to this distinction, despite the open-ended understanding of development put forward in 1967 by Paul VI in *Populorum Progressio*, and the acceptance by Paul VI a few years later in *Octogesima Adveniens* that in the face of widely varying situations we must not aim 'to put forward a solution which has universal validity' (*OA*, 4). Consequently, there is still a real danger that Catholic social teaching may not give sufficient emphasis to some of the most fundamental values of non-Western cultures; for instance, serenity, respect, gentleness, harmony, cooperation, rootedness, contemplation, and a sense of oneness with nature or with 'the All'. If the contemplative ecological spirituality put forward in *Laudato Si'* is fully accepted, it will provide a vital safeguard against this danger.

A fifth area in which Catholic social teaching is somewhat weak or undeveloped concerns the issue of *alternatives* to the present model of development. This is closely related to the previous point. It is understandable – though inexcusable – that *politicians* should play down the problems associated with a reliance on rapid economic Western-style development as a solution to problems of poverty, inequity, and unemployment. But it is more difficult to understand why so few Church leaders at the local level have taken seriously the sharp criticism by recent popes – above all by Pope Francis – as well as by a growing number of economists and other scientists, of the present model of development. The world needs to be forcefully reminded how futile and foolish it is to imagine that more economic growth can solve the major economic problems that face all of us.[1] Furthermore, the popes and other Church leaders need to go beyond their call for a change of lifestyle and for frugality by those who are well off. They need to spell out practical ways in which people can live more simply, less exploitatively, and more in partnership with nature. Pope Francis, in his ecological encyclical has taken an important step in this direction by

---

1   See the comprehensive study by Kirby and O'Mahony, for instance, pp. 102–3, 107, 117, 125, 127, 196, and all of chapter nine on what the authors call 'ecosocialism'.

praising small-scale alternative approaches, and indicating various ways in which people can and should live more simply.

It is particularly important that Church leaders should offer moral and practical support to those committed Christians and others who are already modelling such an alternative lifestyle. Perhaps it is not too much to expect that Church leaders should find ways in which they themselves can model a pattern of living that is ecologically sustainable and that does not require more than an equitable share of the limited resources of the earth. This may be dismissed as unrealistic. But since the Church is called to be prophetic it has to be somewhat unrealistic. It cannot allow the prevailing situation to be the sole determinant of what is considered realistic.

The sixth area in which Catholic social teaching needs further development and clarification has to do with the role of the Church in politics. The Church has developed some general guidelines over the past one hundred years. Central to the accepted approach is a practical distinction between the area of politics and that of religion – even though the two overlap to some extent. Within the terms of this distinction, the Church's main concern is with religion, but by its nature this includes some involvement in the social and political spheres of life. It is accepted that Church leaders are not entitled to claim any special competence in purely political matters. Lay Christians, in their capacity as citizens, are encouraged to take part in politics, even party politics. The Church discourages priests and members of religious communities from becoming actively involved in overtly political activity, or party politics; the aim is to ensure that the Church does not compromise its basic function by becoming too closely identified with any particular party.

These guidelines have served the Church well and are not to be discarded lightly. But they still leave some awkward questions – particularly since Church leaders have committed the Church to the defence of poor and oppressed people and of the earth. When Church leaders speak out on justice issues they enter the political area. The distinction between politics in a broad sense and party politics is very helpful where a number of different democratic parties, sharing the same fundamental moral values, differ in regard to priorities and programmes; the Church can then maintain its neutrality in relation to all of them. But what happens if there are two major parties and the policy of one of them is to maintain an unjust and totally undemocratic social order while the other party is committed to social justice? What if a tyrannical government outlaws democratic opposition and the only effective resistance is through movements that the oppressive government labels subversive? What about a situation where the leader of a government denies that humans are the main cause of our ecological problems, and deliberately dismantles the laws and regulations which had been enacted to protect the environment? If Church leaders speak out clearly and specifically on issues of justice and care for the earth in such situations, they will be understood to be taking sides on political issues. They will in effect no longer be keeping aloof from party politics. Pope Francis is clearly aware of this issue and he has not hesitated to encourage social and political activists to challenge the present unjust world order. Official teaching ought to follow his lead in taking explicit account of such situations.

The seventh area in which Catholic social teaching needs to be developed is in developing a more comprehensive style of social analysis. Church authorities have tended to shy away from the question of the class structure of society. This springs from an understandable desire not to foment class struggle. But the consequence is that Church leaders often fail to take full account of the conflicting interests of the rich and the poor. Pope Francis has been blunt in his condemnation of the exploitative model of capitalism that is dominant at present and in showing how it damages developing countries. But there is need for an even more explicit and specific condemnation of particular ways in which present-day neo-colonialism is perpetuating, and in some respects exacerbating, the exploitation and injustice which were at the heart of the colonialism of the past. And there is need for other Church leaders to follow Francis in opposing this system.

An eighth point on which the teaching of the Church remains insufficiently developed is related to the previous one; it concerns the question of confrontation and conflict. Traditional social teaching put so much emphasis on harmony and consensus that it played down the fact that confrontation can at times be an essential aspect of working for social justice. The early teaching of John Paul II on solidarity provided a partial corrective for this oversight. But up to quite recently priests or members of religious communities who help the poor in organising themselves to press for their rights have often been frowned upon or condemned as being too political or as being involved in a suspect form of liberation theology. Hopefully this will change as the more liberationist approach of Pope Francis permeates into the Church as a whole. His encouragement of social activists who have 'the smell of the struggle' represents a quite radical change of emphasis in Catholic social teaching.

A ninth issue on which there is need for development in Catholic social teaching is one where Church teaching on personal sexual morality intersects with wider social issues. This is the topic of the population explosion. The immediate issues that need to be addressed are not mainly the sheer size of the global population, which is now in excess of seven billion. There are two more pressing issues. The first of these is the vicious circle in which the population of very poor countries find themselves. Huge numbers of poor people are living in situations where they do not have reliable health services or government-provided social services. Consequently, many children die in infancy, and those who survive and prosper are expected to support their younger siblings and relatives, as well as their aging parents. The resulting rapid growth in population undermines governmental development plans in poor countries and leads to intolerable pressure on environmental resources.

The second pressing population issue that needs to be addressed is the number of people in the Western world augmented by the rapidly increasing number of people in many developing countries that are now living a more Western lifestyle. The extravagance of both of these groups is putting a greatly increased demand on the limited resources of planet earth. The ecological encyclical of Pope Francis has gone quite some way toward stressing the urgency of this latter issue.

Governments in poor countries, faced with population growth that seems almost out of control, need to adopt an ecologically sustainable model of development that gives priority to the elimination of poverty and that provides people with some adequate level of healthcare and of social security. And they can only do this if the wealthier countries provide them with adequate funding to enable them to adopt a type of development that respects the environment. In his ecological encyclical, Pope Francis has stressed this point by exploring the reality of what he calls 'ecological debt' (*LS,* 51). There is need for other Church leaders to follow his lead, and for theologians to spell out more fully the social teaching of the Church on this issue.

However, this still leaves us with the question whether particular forms of contraception are morally acceptable. The Vatican's consistent refusal to rethink the condemnation of contraception in *Humanae Vitae* has meant that Church authorities are reluctant to make a serious examination of the problems arising from rapid population growth in many developing countries. As I noted in chapter twenty-three, on one occasion Francis responded to a question by suggesting that, in his view, it could be morally acceptable for a woman to use contraception to protect herself against rape or violence. This might perhaps be a significant step in a move towards a softening of the official Church position that artificial contraception is always wrong.

One particular issue in this regard is whether a person (usually a woman) is justified in using contraception as protection against infection from a sexual partner who is carrying the HIV/AIDS virus. This is a particularly serious issue in poor countries. Many of these countries have lost a high proportion of their badly needed professional people (healthcare workers, teachers, etc.). Furthermore, the rapid growth in the number of AIDS orphans has overwhelmed the ability of the traditional extended family support system to cope. The Catholic Church has responded magnificently in providing health services, health education programmes, and care for orphans. But in this area, too, the strong stand of the official Church against contraception leads to a reluctance to examine the whole issue from a wider perspective.

All this leads on to the bigger issue of whether the Catholic Church needs a much more radical rethink of its whole theology of sexuality. For generations the main basis for the official Church teaching on most moral issues – and particularly on issues of sexual morality – has been the 'natural law' tradition. There is no doubt that this is a very valuable tradition. But in recent times many serious moral theologians have come to believe that the Church has gotten itself trapped into a particular outdated understanding of 'natural law'. They would argue for a different understanding of natural law. They would say that it is a mistake to base our moral judgements on an examination of the nature of each particular organ – the eye, the ear, the sexual organs, etc. – as if each of them were a distinct machine with its own inbuilt purpose. Instead we should make our moral judgements in terms of the nature of the human person as a whole – what is right or wrong for this person to do in this situation. They believe that this could lead to the development of a more human and genuine sexual ethics based on living a virtuous life, in which a responsible use of contraception would be permissible, perhaps even necessary. And this in turn would open up the possibility of a rethink of what it means for LGBT people to live morally.

On all these issues the emphasis of Pope Francis on discernment and conscientious decision-making leads to what one might call 'a pastoral softening' in the application of official Church teaching. But this would still leave an unduly wide gap between objective and subjective morality.

A tenth issue on which the social teaching of the Church is in need of further development concerns the question of *justice within the Church itself.* Prior to the coming of Pope Francis, the only major document in which this issue was taken up courageously was the document 'Justice in the World', which was issued by the Synod of Bishops of 1971. It recognised that if the Church's social teaching about society is to be credible and effective, then the Church must be a living witness to this teaching.

For perhaps twenty-five years prior to the papacy of Pope Francis, serious questions were being raised about the way authority was being exercised in the Catholic Church. The Vatican curia had largely reduced the bishops to the role of line managers. Many diocesan bishops were not sharing authority adequately with their priests. Many local pastors were not allowing lay Christians (especially women) effective participation in decision-making. The radically new approach of Pope Francis has given hope that all this can change. From the beginning he made it quite clear that he wanted to share decision-making at the highest level with the bishops. And his repeated sharp condemnation of clericalism shows his determination to do all he can to ensure that this kind of participatory decision-making will operate at every level of Church life. Particularly striking is his statement in *Evangelii Gaudium*: 'Since I am called to put into practice what I ask of others, I too must think about a conversion of the papacy' (*EG,* 32).

A further issue in relation to justice in the Church concerns the use of sexist language in most of its official documents and especially in the texts of the liturgy. Many people, above all in the English-speaking world, are quite shocked at the reluctance of the Vatican to use more inclusive language, especially in liturgical texts. They also point to other instances of what they see as sexism in the Church. Some go much further and accuse the official Church of being grossly patriarchal in its organisation and mode of acting.

The eleventh and final lacuna in the social teaching of the Catholic Church has to do not so much with *what* it is teaching but rather with the *process* through which the teaching is worked out and articulated. In recent years, the Vatican has begun to consult lay experts more frequently. But private consultation with specialists is not sufficient. The basic point is that Church authorities at all levels must find more effective ways of listening to the *sensus fidei*; that is, the deep Christian beliefs and convictions of the laity. People expect to be consulted about matters that touch their own lives. Many Catholics would like to be actively involved in the formulation of the Church's social teaching. They have much to contribute. Church leaders should make special efforts to find ways of listening more effectively to the voices of people who are poor, of young people, and of women.

Charles Curran offers some helpful ideas on this topic:

> The hierarchical Magisterium is not only an authoritative teacher ... it is also a learner. This hierarchical office does not simply possess the necessary moral truths in its 'sacred

patrimony'. It is searching continually for the moral truth ... and testing this truth in broader dialogue with all human sources of moral wisdom and knowledge and all people of good will. (Curran 2002, 116)

Since this is the case, Church leaders should acknowledge that the Holy Spirit speaks through many voices and should welcome the new light which comes from a wide variety of sources, from inside and outside the Church. As Curran points out, 'A more open and consultative process would ensure the truly authoritative nature of the teaching' (2002, 118).

Pope Francis has made clear that he favours a participatory or consultative approach. A very significant move toward such an approach was his insistence that part of the preparation for the Synods of Bishops in 2014 and 2015 should be the preparation of a questionnaire to be sent to bishops all over the world with the request that it would be used to ascertain the views of Christians on the ground. It is true that the actual content of the questionnaires left much to be desired. And in some dioceses the consultation was very inadequate. But the questionnaires were a first step that signalled the possibility – even the likelihood – of much more effective participation and consultation at every level of the Church.

Chapter Twenty-Five

Bridge-Builder

The principal title which has been given to popes in recent centuries is 'Supreme Pontiff', which is the English version of the Latin *Pontifex Maximus*. This is not the kind of title that Pope Francis would wish to use. He prefers to call himself 'the Bishop of Rome'. So it is rather ironic that in its literal meaning the word *pontifex* ('pontiff') means 'bridge-builder' – and that is very much the role that Francis sees himself as called to play in the Church and in the wider world.

Francis played a key role in defusing the sixty-year stand-off between Cuba and the USA. And in several of his overseas visits – for instance in his November 2015 visit to the Central African Republic – he has striven to promote reconciliation between warring factions. He also invited Israeli President Shimon Peres and Palestinian President Mahmoud Abbas to visit him in the Vatican, where he hosted joint prayers with them.

We have a good example of the approach of Pope Francis to bridge-building in the response he gave to a question he was asked on the flight back to Rome from Bangladesh on 2 December 2017. He was asked whether he regretted the fact that he had not used the controversial word 'Rohingya' when he was in Myanmar a few days earlier. In reply he said, 'Your question is very interesting because it leads me to reflect on the way I try to communicate. For me, the most important thing is that the message arrives.' He pointed out that he had used the word on previous occasions and that [in Myanmar] he had made clear where he stood by speaking of the right to citizenship in which nobody is excluded. He then went on to say that he knew that, if he had used the Rohingya word in an official address, his message would not have got through. He added that while he did not have the pleasure of slamming the door by making a denunciation, he did have the satisfaction of knowing that his message had been heard – and that it had continued to be heard right up to the time he did use the word when actually speaking with the Rohingya refugees in Bangladesh.

As I pointed out in chapter eight, Francis has been a particularly committed bridge-builder in his relationships with other Christian churches. One thinks, for instance, of his exceptionally close relationship with the Eastern Orthodox Patriarch Bartholomew of Constantinople, his meeting in February 2016 in Havana, Cuba with Patriarch Kirill of Moscow, and of his taking part in an Orthodox Liturgy with Patriarch Karekin II, the Catholicos of the Armenian Apostolic Church in June 2016. In April 2017, during his visit to Egypt, Francis and the Coptic Pope Tawadros II signed a common declaration in which Catholics and Copts declared for the first time that they will recognise each other's sacrament of Baptism. One thinks also of his friendly meetings with the Anglican Archbishop Justin Welby, of his trip to Sweden in October 2016 where he hugged Rev. Martin Junge, General Secretary of the Lutheran World Federation, and shared prayer with Lutheran Archbishop Antje Jackelén, Primate of the Church of Sweden, and of his surprisingly warm and close relationship with Pentecostal leaders.

Close cooperation between Christians and people of other religions is a very high priority for him – and he has shown the way himself. For many years he has had a close friendship with Rabbi Abraham Skorka with whom he co-wrote a book. On his visit to the Western Wall in Jerusalem, in May 2017, he was accompanied not only by Rabbi Skorka but also by his other friend, the Muslim leader Omar Abboud. In Bangladesh on 1 December 2016 he asked Christians to 'work unremittingly to build bridges and to foster dialogue, for these efforts not only facilitate communication between different religious groups, but also awaken the spiritual energies needed for the work of nation building in unity, justice and peace'.

BRIDGE-BUILDING IN CATHOLIC SPIRITUALITY

At the present time there are damaging divisions within the Catholic Church and yawning gaps in the spirituality practised and fostered by different groups of Catholics. In Bangladesh on 2 December 2017, speaking to priests, religious sisters and brothers and novices, Pope Francis said that as well as having harmony between religions, the Church also has to be an example of harmony within itself; and he added that there are many enemies to harmony within the Church. It is clear that he sees it as an important aspect of his ministry as pope to bridge these gaps.

For many people, including quite a number of Catholic leaders, the words 'evangelisation' and 'mission' have a restricted meaning. They believe that their call to be evangelisers means mainly encouraging Catholics to be more fervent, inviting non-practising Catholics to return to the sacraments and to a life of prayer and works of charity, and also inviting non-Catholics to embrace the Catholic religion. On the other hand, there are many deeply committed Catholics whose understanding of evangelisation centres mainly on care of the earth and working for justice in society. If this was just a difference of emphasis it could be a healthy tension in the Church, and perhaps even within individual Christians. But unfortunately these different concepts of evangelisation often cause mutual incomprehension and lead to recriminations and negative judgements between Catholics even within parishes and religious communities.

Closely related to these differences on the meaning of evangelisation is the very serious division between Catholics who have two different views about the pastoral priorities of the Catholic Church. There are many Catholic leaders and committed Catholics 'on the ground' who take the view that abortion is such a serious evil in our world that the Church must give absolute priority to it over all other aspects of its ministry. On the other hand, there are many who believe that opposition to abortion should be one important strand, but not the only one, in a 'seamless garment' approach to protection of life. They want the Church to take a strong stand against abortion, but also against capital punishment, war, and the poverty, oppression and abuse which leaves some women feeling that their only way to survive is to abort their child. They also want the Church to campaign against the injustices in society which cause such poverty and abuse – and to take a leading role in caring for the earth, since for them the 'seamless garment' approach to the protection of life extends also to non-human creatures.

Those who locate themselves on what is commonly seen as the more 'liberal' side on these issues generally feel that Pope Francis is on 'their' side. Conversely, many of those who take a more 'conservative' stance often feel let down, perhaps even betrayed, by what Pope Francis has said and done. The reality is that Pope Francis has made every effort to bridge the gap between these two outlooks. On the evangelisation issue he has undoubtedly taken a position which owes much to liberation theology and action on ecological issues. But he has also laid great stress on the more obviously religious and spiritual aspects of evangelisation. For instance, on 3 June 2017 he joined with thirty thousand singing and clapping Charismatics and Pentecostals in the Roman Circus Maximus, praying with them for a fresh outpouring of the Holy Spirit. And on the protection of life issue he has, as I pointed out in chapter three, taken a strong stand against abortion.

Unfortunately, there are many people who fail to welcome this bridge-building approach of the Pope. It would appear that they are unwilling to bear the discomfort of following the Pope's lead in constructing a bridge or in crossing the bridge to experience something of the outlook of those on the other side. So they tend to reinforce their own prejudices by focusing only on the aspects of his actions and words which fit in comfortably with their own agendas. Furthermore, the people on either side of these divides sometimes exaggerate the differences between the stances of Pope Francis and those of Pope Benedict and Pope John Paul II.

JUSTICE AND ECOLOGY

A quite striking instance of the commitment of Francis to bridging gaps has been his insistence throughout his papacy on the inseparable link between justice issues and ecological issues. This linkage is a central point in his encyclical *Laudato Si'*. Here he repeatedly links care for the earth with work to overcome poverty by challenging the present unjust structures in society; and he spells out this link in some detail. Of course he was not the first to link these two issues, as is shown by the fact that in recent years the term 'ecojustice' has come into widespread use. But Francis has given us a particularly memorable phrase (which he borrowed from Leonardo Boff) when he calls us passionately to hear 'the cry of the earth and the cry of the poor'.

OBJECTIVE VERSUS SUBJECTIVE

One of the widest gaps in the Catholic Church at this time is related to two different aspects of Christian faith. On the one hand it is essential that the Church should continue to preach its fundamental doctrines and that it should not play down traditional Church morality and the validity of its own Church laws. On the other hand, the Church insists on the sanctity of personal conscience and the subjective aspect of morality. This issue has led to major controversy and division in the Church on the question of whether or not divorced and remarried Catholics might, in some circumstances, receive Holy Communion; but the same issue arises overtly or implicitly in regard to various other aspects of Church doctrine and Church laws.

Once again, Francis has sought to be a bridge-builder on this issue. He has distinguished clearly between objective truth and morality on the one hand and on the other hand the need to take account of personal conscience. For him, the Christian faith must not be seen as just a set of truths, existing in the abstract, almost like an ideology. Faith is a personal response which is evoked in the depths of an individual as he or she exists at that time, with all the inadequacies of the person as well as all the person's positive qualities.

By insisting again and again on the importance of *discernment* Francis emphasises the link between the objective and subjective aspects of faith. The point is that authentic decisions about what to believe or what action is morally correct in a given situation cannot be made lightly or impulsively or based on one's immediate desires. The person must reflect seriously on the teachings, the traditions, and the laws of the Church and must pray for guidance on how best to apply them in the person's present situation. Francis suggests that in doing this the person can and should be assisted by a qualified and sympathetic pastor. And for Francis this joint discernment is a crucial aspect of the pastoral ministry of priests and spiritual directors. Furthermore, he insists that *communal* discernment is important in the life of every community and in Church life at every level – papal, diocesan, and parish. His view on this issue is undoubtedly affected not only by his own pastoral experience but also by his Jesuit spirituality and training.

Francis also believes and insists that in communities at every level, God has given those who are poor or on the margins a special role. For him, the 'poor' (in every sense of that word) have deeper insight into the truths of faith. In this context he believes that women have a major contribution to make to the life of the Church and to the practice of the Christian faith.

CONCLUSION

It is obvious that Pope Francis has strong views about many changes he wishes to bring about in the Catholic Church and in the spirituality of committed Christians. One might have thought that he could be tempted to push these changes through on his own authority. However, one of his strongest beliefs is that the Catholic Church should practise collegiality, synodality and dialogue at every level. This means that he has to listen to the views of others, take account of different opinions, perhaps adapt his own views and try to bring people along with him in whatever changes he believes are still needed. So he has to balance his desire for changes with his commitment to practise authentic dialogue – and has to take the time required to do so.

So far, Francis has succeeded quite well in carrying through much of what I have been calling his 'agenda'. He has done so despite the strong resistance of a relatively small but fairly influential group of hard-line Church leaders and conservative Catholics. What is the secret of his remarkable success in carrying such a large proportion of Catholics with him – at least to a point where they believe that he is leading the Church in the right direction? And how is it that, even though he poses such a radical challenge to the unjust economic and political structures of our world, he is admired and looked up to by so many people of other religions or of none?

I think there are two main reasons for this. First of all, one has the sense that in his formal speeches and documents, as well as in his more informal interviews and conversation, he is not just repeating material that has been drafted for him by others. It is obvious that he personally believes in everything he says – and frequently this belief of his is quite passionately expressed.

Secondly, we can see that he speaks from the heart. He is in touch with his heart, with his deep feelings, and this is what enables him to make contact at a deep level with the people he meets. His reactions, his words and his actions are not based on theories or ungrounded ideas; they are always pastoral, directly in relation to the specific situation of those with whom he is relating. For instance, it was obvious that he was very deeply moved when he met and spoke with a group of Rohingya refugees in Bangladesh; and he was willing to let that be seen. It is because he is so in touch with his heart that he is keenly aware of the sensitivities of each situation in which he finds himself and is able to respond spontaneously in an appropriate way. His special gift is heart-to-heart communication.

Of course, behind this is his deep Christian faith and love, grounded in long hours of prayer. He has made no secret of the fact that he believes he has been guided by the Holy Spirit in a particular way from the very first moments of his election as pope. He trusts the Spirit and seems quite assured that his spontaneous response to each person and each situation does not simply spring from personal impulses but is in tune with where the Spirit is leading him. In this, as in so much else, he is a model for all of us. We have every reason to believe that his papacy is a *kairos* time for the Christian churches and, hopefully, for the wider world.

Bibliography

DOCUMENTS AND ADDRESSES OF POPE FRANCIS AND
RELATED VATICAN DOCUMENTS
(in chronological order)*

Address to Journalists, 16 March 2013.

Homily at Inaugural Mass, 19 March 2013.

Audience with the Diplomatic Corps accredited to the Holy
See, 22 March 2013.

Homily at Chrism Mass on Holy Thursday, 28 March 2013.

Urbi et Orbi Message, Easter Sunday, 31 March 2013.

General Audience, 5 June 2013.

Homily in Lampedusa, 8 July 2013.

Meeting with Bishops of Brazil, 28 July 2013.

Interview with Antonio Spadaro, SJ, 30 September 2013;
americamagazine.org.

Apostolic Exhortation Evangelii Gaudium, 24 November 2013.

Dialogue with Leaders of USG. The dialogue took place on 29
November 2013. Original text of Fr Spadaro's account of the
dialogue published in Italian in La Civiltá Cattolica, 2014, I,
3–17; English translation by Fr Donal Mardari, SJ, revised
January 6, 2014; laciviltacattolica.it.

Address to the New Ambassadors accredited to the Holy See, 12
December 2013.

Message for World Day of Peace 2014.

*All items available on The Holy See website (w2.vatican.va) unless otherwise stated.

Letter to those who will be created Cardinals at the Consistory of 22 February, 12 January 2014.

Agreement to Eradicate Human Trafficking signed at the Vatican, 17 March 2014; zenit.org.

Letter to Cardinal Lorenzo Baldisseri, 1 April 2014.

Address to Conference on Combatting Human Trafficking, 10 April 2014; news.va.

Letter to Participants in 19th International Congress of Association of Penal Law and of 3rd Congress of Latin-American Association of Penal Law and Criminology, 30 May 2014.

Message for World Mission Day, 8 June 2014.

Address to Archbishop Justin Welby, 16 June 2014.

Address in University of Molise, 5 July 2014.

Dialogue with Journalists on Flight Back to Rome from Korea, 18 August 2014; news.va.

Address to Civil Leaders in Albania, 21 September 2014.

Interim Report of Rapporteur to Synod, 13 October 2014.

Final Report of the 2014 Session of the Synod, 18 October 2014.

Address to Delegates of the International Association of Penal Law, 23 October 2014.

Address to the Participants of the World Meeting of Popular Movements, 28 October 2014. In the text of the present book this address is referred to as *Movements*.

Address to the European Parliament in Strasbourg, 25 November 2014.

Message of 27 November 2014 to the President of the 20th Conference of States Party to the United Nations Framework Agreement on Climate Change, Lima, Peru, 1–12 December 2014; news.va.

Address to the Members of the International Theological Commission, 5 December 2014.

Address to Members of the Vatican Curia, 22 December 2014.

Message for World Day of Peace, 1 January 2015.

Address to Participants in the Plenary Assembly of the Pontifical Council for Culture, 7 February 2015.

In-flight Press Conference from the Philippines to Rome, 19 February 2015.

Letter to Catholic University of Argentina, 10 March 2015; zenit.org.

Letter to the President of the International Commission against the Death Penalty, 20 March 2015.

Bull of Indiction of the Jubilee Year of Mercy, *Misericordiae Vultus*, 11 April 2015.

Endorsement by Pope Francis of Petition of the Global Catholic Climate Movement, 6 May 2015; ncronline.org.

Homily at the Mass for the Opening of the Caritas Internationalis General Assembly, 12 May 2015; ncronline.org.

Encyclical *Laudato Si'*, 24 May 2015.

Address to Participants in 39th Session of FAO, 11 June 2015.

Address to Educators, Quito, 7 July 2015.

Address to Participants in the Second World Meeting of Popular Movements, Santa Cruz de la Sierra, Bolivia, 9 July 2015.

Message to Participants in Conference in Rome on Mining, 18 July 2015.

Address to Participants in a Meeting on Sustainable Development, 11 September 2015.

Message for World Day of Migrants and Refugees 2016, 12 September 2015.

Homily at Shrine of Our Lady of Cobre, Santiago, Cuba, 22 September 2015.

Address to US Congress, Washington, DC, 24 September 2015.

Address to the General Assembly of the United Nations, New York, 25 September 2015.

Introductory Remarks to Synod Fathers, 5 October 2015.

Address to Commemorate the 50th Anniversary of the Institution of the Synod of Bishops, 17 October 2015.

Final Report of the Synod of Bishops, 24 October 2015.

Address at the Conclusion of the Synod, 24 October 2015.

Homily at Ciudad Juárez, Mexico, 17 February 2016.

In-flight Press Conference on Return Journey from Mexico to Rome, 17 February 2016.

Post-synodal Apostolic Exhortation *Amoris Laetitia*, 19 March 2016.

Message to Cardinal Peter KA Turkson on the Occasion of the Conference on 'Non-violence and Just Peace: Contributing to the Catholic Understanding of and Commitment to Non-violence', 6 April 2016.

Conference on 'Non-violence and Just Peace: Contributing to the Catholic Understanding of and Commitment to Non-violence', Rome, 11–13 April 2016.

In-flight Press Conference on Flight from Lesbos to Rome, 16 April 2016.

Address to the International Union of Superiors General (UISG), 12 May 2016.

In-flight Press Conference on Flight from Sweden to Rome, 1 November 2016.

Interview with TV2000, 21 November 2016; en.radiovaticana. va/news/2016/11/21/pope_recalls_mercy_fridays,_jubilee_in_ tv2000_interview/1273670

Message for 50th World Day of Peace, 'Non-violence: a Style of Politics for Peace', 8 December 2016.

General Audience, 8 February 2017.

Message for the 104th World Day of Migrants and Refugees 2018, 15 August 2017.

Apostolic Letter *Magnum Principium*, 3 September 2017; press.vatican.va/content/salastampa/en/bollettino/pubblico/2017/09/09/170909a.html

Address to Participants in the Meeting Promoted by the Pontifical Council for Promoting the New Evangelisation, 11 October 2017.

Address at FAO on World Food Day, 16 October 2017.

Address to Meeting of New Evangelisation Council, 11 October 2017.

Letter to Cardinal Sarah, 22 October 2017; zenit.org/articles/liturgy-popes-letter-to-cardinal-sarah-unabridged-translation/

Speech to COMECE Conference in Rome, 28 October 2017.

Speech to the Participants in an International Symposium, 'Prospects for a World Free of Nuclear Weapons and for Integral Disarmament', 10 November 2017.

Announcement of New Section in Secretariat of State, November 2017.

Address to Priests, Religious and Consecrated Men and Women, Seminarians and Novices, Bangladesh, 2 December 2017.

Press Conference on Flight Back to Rome from Bangladesh, 2 December 2017.

Address to Members of the Italian Theological Association, 29 December 2017.

Address to Members of the Diplomatic Corps, 8 January 2018.

Address to Authorities, the Civil Society and the Diplomatic Corps, Chile, 16 January 2018.

Address to Priests, Consecrated Men and Women and Seminarians, Chile, 16 January 2018.

Declaration of the Director of the Holy See Press Office, Greg Burke, 16 January 2018; press.vatican.va/content/salastampa/en/bollettino/pubblico/2018/01/16/180116c.html

Address to Indigenous People of Amazonia, Puerto Maldonado, Peru, 19 January 2018.

Address for the Marian Celebration – Our Lady of the Gate, Trujillo, Peru, 20 January 2018.

Press Conference on the Return Flight from Lima to Rome, 21 January 2018.

Address to Representatives of the Yazidi Community in Germany, 24 January 2018.

Address to Official Tribunal of the Roman Rota, 29 January 2018.

Press Release from Vatican Press Office, 30 January 2018; press.vatican.va/content/salastampa/en/bollettino/pubblico/2018/01/30/180130c.html

Report in *National Catholic Reporter* (NCR) on Letter re Abuse by Bishop Barros Given to Pope Francis in 2015, 5 February 2018; ncronline.org/news/accountability/pope-francis-received-sex-abuse-victims-letter-contradicting-denial

Address to Members of the 'Santa Marta Group', 9 February 2018.

Report in NCR on Lecture by Cardinal Cupich, 9 February 2018; ncronline.org/news/theology/cupich-says-amoris-laetitia-changes-how-church-teaches-families-learning

Report by John L. Allen re Bishop Barros in Chile, 9 February 2018; cruxnow.com/news-analysis/2018/02/09/abuse-scandal-pope-stakes-case-evidence-not-authority/

Report in NCR of a dialogue of Pope Francis with Jesuits in Peru on 19 January 2018, 15 February 2018; ncronline.org/news/accountability/pope-francis-says-he-meets-almost-weekly-abuse-victims

Declaration of the Director of the Holy See Press Office, Greg Burke, 15 February 2018; press.vatican.va/context/salastampa/en/bollettino/pubblico/2018/02/13/180215b.html

Letter *Placuit Deo* on Certain Aspects of Christian Salvation, Congregation for the Doctrine of the Faith, 22 February 2018.

Letter of Pope Francis to the Bishops of Chile, 8 March 2018.

Apostolic Exhortation *Gaudete et Exsultate*, 19 March 2018.

SECONDARY SOURCES

Atkinson, Anthony. 2015. *Inequality: What Can be Done?* Cambridge, MA: Harvard University Press.

Bergin, Liam. 2017. 'Translations matter – on Pope Francis's *Magnum Principium*.' *The Furrow*, vol. 68, no. 11 (November 2017): 603–10.

Berry, Thomas. 1978. *The New Story* (Teilhard Studies, no. 1, Winter 1978). Chambersburg, PA: Anima Books.

Berry, Thomas. 1988. *The Dream of the Earth*. San Francisco: Sierra Club Books.

Boff, Leonardo. 1997. *Cry of the Earth, Cry of the Poor*. Maryknoll, NY: Orbis Books.

Boff, Leonardo. 2014. *Francis of Rome and Francis of Assisi: A New Springtime for the Church*. Maryknoll, NY: Orbis Books.

Bollier, David. 2014. *Think Like a Commoner: A Short Introduction to the Life of the Commons*. Gabriola Island, BC: New Society Publishers.

Byrne, Patrick H. 2009. 'What is an Evolutionary Explanation? Darwin and Lonergan.' *Lonergan Workshop*, vol. 23, edited by Fred Lawrence, 13–57. Boston College.

Capra, Fritjof. 2015. '*Laudato Si*': The Ecological Ethics and Systemic Thought of Pope Francis.' 22 June 2015; fritjofcapra.net.

Daly-Denton, Margaret. 2017. *John: An Earth Bible Commentary: Supposing Him to be the Gardener.* London: Bloomsbury.

Delio, Ilia. 2011. *The Emergent Christ: Exploring the Meaning of Catholic in an Evolutionary Universe.* Maryknoll, NY: Orbis Books.

Dorling, Danny. 2014. *Inequality and the 1%.* London: Verso Books.

Feehan, John. 2010. *The Singing Heart of the World: Creation, Evolution and Faith.* Dublin: The Columba Press; and Maryknoll: Orbis Books, 2012.

Feehan, John. 2015. 'Creation, Evolution and Faith: Reflections on the Presence of God in Creation' (privately published).

Feehan, John. 2016. *The Dipper's Acclaim and Other Essays.* Navan: Columban Ecological Institute.

Feehan, John. 2017. 'Creation as Incarnation: Reflections on Biodiversity in *Laudato Si*'.' Sean McDonagh (ed.). 2017. *Laudato Si': An Irish Response.* Dublin: Veritas, 55–82.

Girard, René. 1989. *The Scapegoat.* Baltimore: Johns Hopkins University Press.

Kirby, Peadar. 2017. 'Pope Francis on Power, Politics and the Techno-Economic Paradigm.' Sean McDonagh (ed.). 2017. *Laudato Si': An Irish Response.* Dublin: Veritas, 225–36.

Kirby, Peadar and Tadhg O'Mahony. 2018. *The Political Economy of Low-Carbon Transition: Pathways Beyond Techno-Optimism.* Palgave Macmillan.

Klein, Naomi. 2014. *This Changes Everything: Capitalism vs. the Climate.* New York: Simon & Schuster; London: Allen Lane.

Lawler, Michael G. and Todd A. Salzman. 2017. 'Pope Francis and His Predecessors – a Remarkable and Unremarked Continuity.' *The Furrow*, vol. 68, no. 11 (November 2017), 579–89.

Levertov, Denise. 1993. *Evening Train*. New York: New Direction Books.

Lonergan, Bernard. [1957] 1992. *Insight: A Study of Human Understanding*, vol. 3 of Frederick E. Crowe and Robert M. Doran (eds). *Collected Works of Bernard Lonergan*. Toronto: University of Toronto Press.

Macy, Joanna and Molly Young Brown. 2014. *Coming Back to Life: The Updated Guide to the Work that Reconnects*. Gabriola Island, BC, Canada: New Society Publishers.

Manne, Robert. 2015. '*Laudato Si'*: A Political Reading.' *The Monthly*, 1 July 2015; themonthly.com.au

McDonagh, Sean. 2016. *On Care for Our Common Home, Laudato Si': The Encyclical of Pope Francis on the Environment*. Maryknoll, NY: Orbis Books.

McDonagh, Sean (ed.). 2017. *Laudato Si': An Irish Response*. Dublin: Veritas.

Michaelson, Jay. 2015. 'Pope Francis' environmental encyclical is even more radical than it appears.' *The Washington Post*, 19 June 2015.

O'Collins, Gerald. 2017. *Lost in Translation: The English Language and the Catholic Mass*. Collegeville: Liturgical Press.

O'Hanlon, Gerry. 2015. 'Catholic Social Teaching and Housing.' *Working Notes [of Jesuit Centre for Faith and Justice]*, issue 76, May 2015, 26–31.

Oliver, Mary. 2017. *Devotions: The Selected Poems of Mary Oliver*. New York: Penguin Press.

Pagola, José Antonio. 2009. *Jesus: An Historical Approximation.* Miami: Convivium Press.

Piketty, Thomas. 2014. *Capital in the Twenty-first Century.* Cambridge, MA: Belknap Press of Harvard University Press.

Piketty, Thomas. 2015. 'A Practical Vision of a More Equal Society.' *The New York Review of Books,* vol. 62, no. 11, 25 June–8 July 2015, 26–9. (A lengthy review of Atkinson 2015.)

Pope Francis. 2016. Giuliano Vigini (ed.). *Care for Creation: A Call for Ecological Conversion.* Maryknoll, NY: Orbis Books.

Rohr, Richard. 2011. 'The Cosmic Christ.' *The Catholic Corner;* youtube.com.

Rohr, Richard. 2107. 'Life is headed somewhere good this Advent.' *National Catholic Reporter,* 2 December 2017; ncronline. org/news/spirituality/soul-seeing/life-headed-somewhere-good-advent?utm_source=Dec%202%20_%20Weekend%20 edition&utm_campaign=cc_120217&utm_medium=email

Trócaire (in association with The Global Catholic Climate Movement). 2017. *Ethical Investments in an Era of Climate Change: a guide to reviewing environmental and social governance of catholic investments*; catholicclimatemovement.global/wp-content/uploads/2017/11/GCCM_Tr%C3%B3caire-Catholic-Toolkit.pdf

Vallely, Paul. 2013. *Pope Francis: Untying the Knots.* New York: Bloomsbury Academic.

Wilkinson, Richard, and Kate Pickett. 2010. *The Spirit Level: Why More Equal Societies Almost Always Do Better (with a New Postscript).* London: Allen Lane.

Williams, Rowan. 2015. 'Embracing Our Limits: The Lessons of *Laudato Si'.*' *Commonweal Magazine,* 9 October 2015, 13–15.